The Forgotten Singer

The Forgotten Singer

The Exiled Sister of I. J. and Isaac Bashevis Singer

A MEMOIR BY MAURICE CARR

The Forgotten Singer: The Exiled Sister of I. J. and Isaac Bashevis Singer
A Memoir by Maurice Carr

White Goat Press, the Yiddish Book Center's imprint
Yiddish Book Center
Amherst, MA 01002
whitegoatpress.org

Printed in the United States of America at The Studley Press, Dalton, MA
10 9 8 7 6 5 4 3 2 1

Paperback ISBN 979-8-9877078-0-7
Hardcover ISBN 979-8-9877078-1-4
Ebook ISBN 979-8-9877078-2-1

Library of Congress Control Number: 2022920713

Cover design by Michael Grinley
Cover illustration photograph of Esther Kreitman (From the Archives of
the YIVO Institute for Jewish Research, New York)

Published in France by Le Bord de L'Eau as *La Famille Singer.*
L'autre Exil – Londres; in Italy by Tre Editori as *La famiglia Singer*; and in
Poland by Fame Art Publishing House as *Singerowie: kolejne wygnanie.*

FOREWORD

"The day of days dawns. I go to Calais. On the dockside I catch sight of Lola wrapped in a sealskin and Hazel in a bright red coat, *The Old Nursery Rhymes* upheld on both palms, descending the gangway of the ferryboat. I rush to meet them, sprain my ankle, and keep running for hugs and kisses."

These are practically the last lines of my father's memoir.

The little girl in the red coat is me, and I still like red.

So here I am sitting in front of a typewiter (only it's a computer), just as I saw my father doing from as far back as I can remember, writing and rewriting the first sentence of his article, throwing the paper away and starting again, the papers flying to their last resting place, the wastepaper basket.

Till the evening before the deadline when he used to take me out in our battered old green car and we drove to the post office, which stayed open all night, to send his article off to the newspaper.

When he retired he didn't have a deadline anymore, but he went on writing, so . . . the paper flew.

One of my first memories of my father is sitting with him, my mother, Lola, and my grandparents Esther and Avrum in my grandparents' house in London. A house I remember as dark, damp, cold, and dreary.

Esther, whom everyone in the family called Hinde, was a dumpy figure always dressed in dark clothes, black hair flaring out on either side of a white part in the middle and blue eyes so pale they were almost transparent. She was a somewhat frightening figure.

To me of course she wasn't the writer Esther Kreitman, sister to Israel, Joshua, and Isaac Bashevis Singer. I knew nothing about her unhappy childhood; I knew nothing about her being the first of the Singer siblings to write.

I was a little girl, and to me she was just Buba. My grandfather Zeida was more jovial.

We used to huddle in front of a fire in the chimney that never seemed to warm anything. If there were sunny days, and there must have been, I don't remember them.

I also don't remember her paying any particular attention to me. Not the rosy-cheeked kind of Jewish grandmother who bakes you apfel strudel.

Come to think of it, she must have regarded me as a disaster, because I was the reason her son married my mother.

Because (and this I know from overheard conversations between my parents) Esther had always thought her son would live with her for the rest of her life, that they would sit together at the kitchen table writing.

So my mother's eruption into their cozy life was a tragedy she never accepted.

This tragedy happened because of the Second World War.

One day A. M. Fuchs, refugee from Vienna and the Anschluss, put on his hat and his gloves and took his daughter Lola along to pay his respects to that other well-known Yiddish writer, Esther Kreitman.

Royalty paying a visit to royalty.

Esther became my grandmother.

My father was bowled over by Lola's beauty and also the chutzpah with which she talked back to her father, he who was always very deferential to his own mother. At the time Lola had a husband who had stayed in Vienna, so Esther thought it safe to suggest her son show her around London. There would be no danger in his having a relationship with a married woman.

8

There she made a fatal mistake.

Because I arrived on the scene. Lola got a divorce, and my father used to describe the scene where, standing in the kitchen where everything important happened, he put his arm around my mother's shoulder, and in those days that meant "We're getting married."

So I was born during the war, not a cheerful time.

Around the chimney fire I remember my mother in the blonde halo of her hair and Esther in the dark frizz of her curls saying nasty things to one another while my father perched uncomfortably on a stool between them, a long, thin, timid, uncertain young man not knowing how to deal with these two female furies, the one feeling she'd rescued him from an overbearing mother, the other that her son had been stolen away from her.

Maurice loved his mother and felt his mission in life was to look after her and protect her, so falling in love with Lola was a bit of a tragedy for him too.

I think he felt guilty about this all his life.

My father during the war had been working for *The Daily Telegraph* and then Reuters and the BBC. One of these asked him to change his name, as Kreitman, they said, was unpronounceable. So he became Maurice Carr. After the war he was sent as a foreign correspondent to Paris.

My father's ambition was to become a writer. Before I was born he had published several books. But because he married and had a child he felt he had to concentrate on being a journalist in order to earn a living.

Of this I have always felt guilty.

Sometime before he died he seemed to relive the scene in Antwerp when he and his mother were on their way to Poland and she fell down in front of a tram foaming at the mouth in an epileptic fit.

And he would weep uncontrollably. My mother and I wouldn't know what to say to comfort him.

Maybe Maurice is now sitting together with Esther at a heavenly kitchen table writing.

To write—that was his main aim in life.

Maurice wrote slowly; it didn't come easily to him, contrary to his uncle Bashevis, from whom the writing seemed to flow.

Maurice had mixed feelings about Bashevis.

I myself only met him three times, but I could see he was a man full of contradictions.

THE FIRST MEETING

The first time I remember meeting my great-uncle Bashevis was at Orly airport in Paris. He wasn't yet the well-known writer, winner of the Nobel Prize, but a Yiddish writer known only to the happy few. He was on his way back from Tel Aviv, where my parents lived and his plane was in transit for New York. He had told my father he would like to meet me.

So I go to Orly and see from afar a man arguing with some sort of official in uniform. I recognize immediately this thin man whose clothes seem to float around his body and the back of whose head has the same massive bulbous shape as that of my father. I go to talk to the customs official and get permission for him to come out of the embarkation zone.

We go to a café, sit down, he turns an icy blue look on me, and says, "I'm not at all interested in family, OK?" It was only years later that I wondered why, if that was the case, he had wanted to meet me.

Then he talks to me about a painting of mine he had seen in my parents' flat and that my father had given him. He had put it in his suitcase. It showed a pious, bearded Jew brooding over an empty chessboard.

My uncle then flew off—

THE SECOND MEETING

The second time I met him was at the reception his Paris editor gave for him after his Nobel Prize. I'd been living in England when he got the prize, and when I heard on the BBC "The Nobel Prize for literature is . . ." I knew seconds before the announcer said it that it would be Isaac Bashevis Singer.

I didn't quite know what I was doing at this reception or who had invited me. I wandered around the room, and every time I glanced toward Bashevis he seemed to be looking at me; his pale blue eyes were like lakes filling up the whole room. I finally went up to where he and Alma were standing and said to Alma, "I'm Hazel."

"I know," she said. "I recognized you. You look just like your grandmother."

Oooh, I wasn't happy to hear that; my grandmother was very short of being a beauty—

THE THIRD MEETING

The third time I met him I was on a visit to New York.

I went to ring at the door of their apartment. It opened. Bashevis stood there, and the first thing he said to me was, "I still have your painting." He started to look for it and eventually found it under a pile of books and magazines.

Then Bashevis took me to lunch in one of the cafeterias he used to go to. Even if one cares nothing about family a niece has to be fed. While we were there people kept coming up and saying how they loved his books. To each one he said the same words: "You have made my day." I took this as ironic, but they took it seriously.

Then I accompanied him through some dark streets. He stopped in front of a house and said goodbye. I was sure he was going to see one of his mistresses.

My father used to tell me that Bashevis had told him that if he wants to be a good writer he should have a mistress who lives on the sixth floor. Climbing all those stairs would be good for the creative adrenaline.

He also one day said to my father, "Your mother was a madwoman." My father didn't speak to him for years after that. Alma wrote a letter saying he didn't always mean what he said and to please forgive him.

Bashevis told me on that street that my father had written to him saying he was going to commit suicide. Bashevis said to me, "I'd rather he'd written to me *after* committing suicide."

That left me voiceless. Later I understood this to mean he would have liked a message from the other side.

I said to him, "Do you think we will meet again?"

He answered, "If God wills it."

God didn't.

by Hazel Karr

1. WORLD WAR 1, THE GREAT WAR

"Take cover! Take cover! Take cover!"

In my sleep I hear the singsong alarm rising to a crescendo, then falling away. And into my dream drifts a silvery fish. I know even before opening my eyes in the dark that its monstrous replicas are afloat in the sky. I know that these overhead fishes are zeppelins and the eggs they drop on London are bombs.

Awake now, it occurs or recurs to me that this voice belongs to the same character who in daylight, riding on a rickety horse and cart, comes whining "Old rags! Old rags! Old rags!" and of whom nobody ever takes any notice. Now he strides through the night changing his tune to "Take cover! Take cover!" and has everybody, everybody, everybody tumbling out of bed. No wonder he sounds pleased with himself, getting his own back with a vengeance.

For my part, snug under my eiderdown, I know I need simply pull it tight over my head to be safe. Buildings are about to topple, people will be crushed or blown to bits, but this isn't going to happen in our little back street, no, not in Henry Road with its tiny gardens in front of every house, which looks exactly like every other house. There is a difference, though; ours is a Jewish shelter home for refugees from Antwerp.

Grown-ups can't help behaving the way they do. Standing in his *gatkes*—long underpants—Papa Avrum shades with one hand the flame of a candle. Because of the blackout no light must show through our uncurtained window. Mama Hindele thrusts my arms into an overcoat and muffles me with a scarf. She and he both put on dressing gowns. And out we step into the gaslit entrance hall.

Already trooping downstairs from the top second floor are the Bronsteins. Of the eight or nine brothers—I just can't get the count right— the joker, who carries a stool for Grandma Rivka, plays the tram conductor: "Standing room only! Fares please!"

Papa Avrum is all smiles. Mama Hindele's wan smile turns sour at the sight of the first-floor Schlesingers, who deposit a straw mat and seat themselves on an upper stair with Ernst squeezed tight and squirming between his black-coated papa and his bejeweled mama. If let loose, he will jump at, play, and wrestle with me.

"Look," murmurs Mama Hindele, "at the vulgar Galicians seated on their throne, who want to keep their prince away from my Moishele!" Knowing how eager I am to play with him, she bends down to me and whispers, "He's big, twice your age, and could hurt you. Not that Herr und Frau Schlesinger would mind. They consider themselves superior because they speak Hochdeutch. Our *mamaloshen*, our Yiddish, if you please, isn't good enough for them."

Mama Hindele's frizzy chestnut hair, divided by a chalk-white parting, bristles like uplifted wings. Her knitted, dark eyebrows twitch and her red eyelids flutter more than usual. With a sigh and a flourish at the outsize, swollen head of poor Ernst she says, softly, "Nebih"—pitiful. The word rings out loud and clear in the hush that has suddenly fallen between two distant thuds.

If a boom comes close enough to shake the walls, we'll all scramble down into the musty cellar. There in the torchlight I'll be scared stiff of the rats. They do nothing worse than brush up against me. I shrink and they scuttle away, sweeping the floor with their whiskers and their long tails. Never once have they bitten me, but that's what they want to do. Their mind—and I see they're all of one mind—is set on chewing me. Bombs maim and kill without really meaning to. They're not alive, not even eggs falling out of the sky from silvery fishes. So I listen to their hit-or-miss drumbeat and am not afraid. As long as I was silly enough to believe that my teddy bear was alive I loved him. Now I know better, but I won't stop loving the Bronsteins' pussycat, Delilah. She's a beauty, always ready to purr and lick her kittens. Maybe rats are so ugly because all they want to do is to eat rubbish and bite people. But how come Ernst pulls such a horrible face when he simply wants to play with me? His gorgeous mama and handsome papa aren't that simple. Looks alone don't tell who should be loved and who should not be loved. The things grown-ups badly—perhaps secretly—want or don't want, that's what counts.

Pleased not only with the walls that don't shake but with my immense wisdom, I rest my head on Papa Avrum's fat thigh, doze off, and even dream till the "All clear!" singsong orders everybody back to bed.

It is Mama Hindele and not Papa Avrum who raises a hand to the holy mezuza on our doorpost and kisses her fingertips. My eiderdown is still warm. I want to pick up my dreams where they broke off, but I never can; it's a lost cause.

I know what to expect when I wake up in the morning. Mama Hindele will still be asleep. Papa Avrum won't hang around to hear her *vilde haloimis,* wild dreams, which she never forgets. His own dreams, if he has any, he keeps to himself. Early every morning he goes off looking for work, any kind of work.

2. THE JEWISH SHELTER

I won't grow up big and strong if I don't swallow the teaspoonful of softboiled egg Mama presses to my lips. It isn't just any egg, it's a rationed egg. "Why the hens can't lay enough eggs in wartime," says Mama, "and why millions of children are starved of bread, never mind eggs, and why men go to war to kill and get killed, God only knows."

When her hand starts to tremble I open my mouth, gulp down teaspoonful after teaspoonful till the shell is empty. I'm full of egg and feel like vomiting.

I climb down from my high chair at the kitchen table and run upstairs to the Bronsteins'. There I can do as I please, which is listen and watch what others are doing. The Bronsteins don't pay any attention to me. They haven't the time. They're in a hurry—I, Moishele, know everything there is to know—in a hurry for the day's business buying and selling diamonds in Hatton Garden. The father, tefillin strapped to his forehead and forearm, stands praying and swaying as fast as he can. The mother stands pouring cup after cup of steaming coffee. The brothers stand eating and drinking.

When they troop downstairs I follow. I find Mama in the bedroom, with her hand in the cupboard where she stores her gifts from Papa's father, Reb Gedalya Kreitman. She lets drop a pearl necklace. I pick it up.

She tries on her fox stole, takes it off, and puts it on again. I know what this means. It means we're going to the Jewish shelter, which—I've heard her say this many times, and she says it again—treats all but the rich refugees from Antwerp like schnorrers, scroungers. So the thing to do for the wife of an out-of-work diamond cutter with no rough diamonds in London for him to cut is to pretend to be rich.

"Look!" Mama says to me. I look at her preening herself. I look at the bare floorboards, at the two iron bedsteads, at the little round table piled high with books, at the wicker armchair, at the two plain chairs, at the flaky whitewashed walls. There's nothing else to look at.

But under the bedcovers, I know, are the lovely eiderdowns that, along with Mama's treasures, Papa carried away from Antwerp when everybody ran away for fear of the bombing. And I clearly remember it happening, even though I was only a tiny baby, because when Mama tells stories I see what she tells me the way I see things in my dreams, except that my dreams are lost moments after I'm awake, leaving only a good or sometimes a bad aftertaste.

I also remember the Manchester Hotel somewhere in London into which the Jewish refugees were packed like sardines in a tin. And I know we might still be there but for Mama's bracelets, necklaces, and fox stole.

I love the ride on a tram and then on a bus to the Jewish shelter. In the crowded waiting room, where we wait and wait, Mama isn't lonely any more. She takes a lively part in the complaints about being kept waiting and about this, that, and the other.

At last it's our turn to be ushered into the office of a frumpy lady, but a real one whom one must address as "Your ladyship." She asks questions in Hochdeutsch without looking up from the papers on her desk. Still, she must have seen the fox stole, because on leaving Mama says with a smile, a real smile, *"Danke schön!"*

Out in the street she fingers the hollows behind my right ear and says, "Moishele, you have her ladyship to thank for your holiday on her land with cows and horses and sheep. But you don't remember, or do you?"

I think and say nothing.

3. MEMORIES

Mama remembers her *vilde haloimis,* her wild dreams. When telling what she has seen in them she doesn't say who the *shaidim*—the devils—are, except that they're from *jene velt*, the other world, come to torment her. I listen, am unhappy, and wish they'd go away.

But I love listening to Mama's stories of people from our own world, from the *alte heim*, her childhood home in Poland. In those moments her eyes, which seem to be gazing at the people back there, blink only once in a while. Her eyebrows are knit; they no longer twitch. Her crinkly hair doesn't bristle away from the chalk-white parting anymore but hangs over her shoulders like a pair of wings at rest.

One day Mama tells me a story I'd never heard before. It's about a czar and Papa. This czar had an army in Russia, and not only did he want Papa to be a soldier in it for twenty-five years but he would also have had to eat pig meat. So my grandfather Reb Gedalya sent Papa, who wasn't yet my Papa, to Antwerp. Who is the czar, and where is Russia? I don't ask, knowing I'll find out if only I keep on listening.

Mama goes to the pile of books on the little round table in the bedroom and picks up three photographs. They're of Papa and Mama in Berlin, where they were married. In one photo they stand side by side. Papa is handsome, important, in a bowler hat, stiff white collar and tie, a smart double-breasted suit, and polished boots. He has sidelocks rolled up into a flourish just under his ears, a curly beard like a fringe the length of his chin, a big moustache, and the twinkle of a smile—he wouldn't be Papa without a smile—in one eye, but in the other eye there's a gleam of mistrust, resentment. Mama is a lady out of a picture book, in a long dress of dark crepe, with a large, white-lace collar tight around the neck overhung by a locket. Her hair doesn't flare—it can't, because it's covered with a wig. And there is to her serene, uptilted face a tinge of mockery.

4. TOSTOO!

As always, Papa Avrum comes home for lunch and, done eating his heaped plate of boiled potatoes and cabbage, accepts Mama Hindele's leftovers. I daren't not finish my own portion, which she has flavored with some butter. I must also drink every drop of my glass of milk.

Over lemon tea Mama Hindele bitterly complains about her life, heaping reproaches on a no-good husband and an irresponsible father who, out of hatred for his own father Reb Gedalya, has never grown up. She goes on and on up to the dread moment when Papa Avrum's persistent smile contorts his whole face and he splutters a thunderous "Tostoo!"

As always she has been telling him that instead of spending his days in idleness, never bringing home a penny, he could act as a *mekler*, diamond broker, for Mr. Bronstein and even for Herr Schlesinger if only he would endear himself to them the way he does to their ladies, those *yahnes*, those busybodies.

Papa Avrum's "Tostoo!" is short for "That's you!" and for the words that fail him to describe Mama Hindele's indecency, her utter shameless pandering to the Reb Gedalyas, the Bronsteins, the Schlesingers of this world, whose hypocrisy and dishonesty, whose mean and greedy lust for self-importance and domination over others, desecrates the earth and stinks to high heaven. Since nothing, just nothing, can be done about it, Papa Avrum is content to do nothing, just nothing, but smile.

If strong feelings that can't be translated into thoughts, let alone words, amount to comprehension, then I, Moishele, do indeed understand both Mama Hindele and Papa Avrum. More's the pity that I have to choose which one I should feel most sorry for.

Now Mama Hindele says something new about the Bronsteins and Herr Schlesinger all being Russian citizens like Papa Avrum and if only he accepted their *protektzia* he could stay home the same as they do and not run off every day into the wilds.

At this Papa Avrum spits a second "Tostoo!" through gritted teeth, shoves his lopsided trilby hat on his head, and walks out.

I balk at my afternoon nap. As much for the sake of comforting Mama as for my own pleasure I recite the alef-beys she has taught me and then try to decipher entire words. After a while she reads me a long-winded but oh so lovely comic *alte heim* story in Yiddish. She says it's by Mendele Moher S'forim, Mendele the Bookseller, not that it's his real name nor does he sell books; he writes them.

Soon after supper I go to bed, fully expecting to hear in my sleep the "Take cover!" call that blots out my dreams. For all the discomfort I know how to relish the fact that everything I foresee actually happens.

5. THE BROTHER

One morning, however, I wake up to the unexpected. The big bed is empty; no sign of Mama Hindele. I go into the kitchen and there she is, but not alone. Papa Avrum, munching bread, sits at the table with his brother Yankel.

Yankel and Papa are twin brothers. I've heard Mama say that one can't tell ordinary twin brothers apart. But she also says that the Kreitmans, common though they are, way below her own family, the Singers, are not ordinary, and there's no likeness, none at all, between Papa Avrum, who hates everyone, and my uncle Yankel, who just loves everyone.

Now they are having breakfast together. On my high stool I sit and look and listen. Somehow I see a secret sort of resemblance between the two brothers because Papa is truly fond of Yankel, at whom he doesn't smile, while Yankel keeps smiling in his shy way as if ashamed of being so different from Papa. He's flimsy, not bulky, and his gaunt face is perched like an outworn shoe on sloping shoulders, not like a pumpkin on broad square shoulders. For all that, the twin brothers belong together, and I wouldn't want to swap my uncle Yankel, whom I dearly love, for my Papa Avrum.

The talk is of their elder brother Laiser, an uncle whom I have never seen because Papa hates him. I know the reason why from Mama's tales. On arrival in Antwerp from Berlin she, Hindele, took off her wig and he, Avrum, shaved off his beard. It was Laiser who told Avrum's father Reb Gedalya of this heresy, and so instead of the promised monthly allowance of many golden rubles they received a letter of many, many curses from this same Reb Gedalya.

My uncle Yankel in his shamefaced way pleads forgiveness for Laiser. But Papa with a big smile and without even a whispered "Tostoo!" will not hear of making peace.

Now suddenly Mama Hindele is in a great hurry; I don't know why. She has me gulp down my egg and my cod liver oil, and no nonsense. Wearing a plain coat and no lipstick, she picks up a large shopping bag and takes me by the hand.

It's Sunday and the church bells are ringing. We take a tram to the East End and, after a long ride, get off where the tram lines end. Together we pause to look round the corner at the broadest street that has ever existed. She says it's called Whitechapel, and I do see some way off what looks like a chapel or a church, but it isn't white. Mama also says that in London this is the street that at the same time most resembles and is most different from Krochmalna, the narrow street where she lived in Warsaw.

I know that in Krochmalna my *zeida*, my grandfather Pinhas Menahem Singer, used to receive a daylong stream of Jews come to ask questions about how to run their lives, how to settle their family problems, how to make the best of their griefs, miseries, and burdens without—heaven forbid!—transgressing the laws of the Torah. Mama says that here in England these same Jews also ask questions—not of their rabbi but of themselves, about how to raise their sons to become doctors and lawyers and how to marry off their daughters to rich men. With one such daughter Yankel is in love, but she won't go under the *hupa*, bridal canopy, with him, though she does let him take her to the Yiddish theater in Whitechapel and for dinner in a kosher restaurant after the show. Yankel is better off staying a bachelor, says Mama Hindele, than having that slut for a wife.

We turn back and go on to The Lane, which isn't a lane at all but an outdoor market stretching on and on, with stall holders all the way yelling their wares in Yiddish or Cockney and wisecracking and haggling with their customers. It's fun, but why does Mama Hindele buy a big plucked chicken and vegetables and fruit? For what celebration is she shopping, I ask. She stops short, stands breathless gazing down at me, and at last answers wryly, "For a fine celebration!"

At home, Papa Avrum and my uncle Yankel are still where we left them, silent, on the same two chairs.

"Why don't you two clowns take the *kindt*, the child, to Finsbury Park? And don't hurry back; I've cooking to do," says Mama Hindele, stuffing crumbs into a paper bag.

After we make it across the traffic of Seven Sisters Road into Finsbury Park, Yankel grasps one hand, Papa Avrum the other, and together they swing me back and forth high up in the air all the way to the pond. It reminds me of how, long ago, Papa Avrum used to carry me, a baby, on his shoulders. I love him, I love my uncle Yankel, I love the long-necked white swans even though their lofty little heads with tight-shut beaks are too deep in thought to pick up the crumbs I throw them. I love the two huge fluffy birds face to face and open-mouthed in the sky, trying to gobble up the sun but melting away because they're only clouds. I love being in Finsbury Park, running around where I please and doing whatever I please. It's never like that when I'm there with Mama Hindele.

Back to Henry Road. The kitchen smells good. Mama Hindele has prepared a perfect Shabbas-like dinner. I eat my fill and for once don't need coaxing to take my afternoon nap. Before I fall asleep Papa Avrum comes and kisses me. This he has never done before. My uncle Yankel also comes to kiss me.

When I wake up it is twilight. I see Mama Hindele sitting with her back to the window, an open book on her lap. I stir and she asks before I can: "Where are Papa and Yankel? They and their elder brother Laiser have gone away. Gone where? To Russia as soldiers. Avrum has left Hindele a *shtroyene vitve,* a grass widow!"

To round off a day of the unexpected, Mama Hindele laughs. Her burst of laughter gives me the shivers.

6. CLEPHANE ROAD

Prim Clephane Road, like prim Henry Road, is lined with gloomy, gray houses outwardly all alike, each with its own little front garden. But indoors, except for the top floor where a Scotland Yard detective lives, one such house is very much like the *alte heim.* There with his family lives Mr. Yakobovich from the shtetl Leoncin, a village by the river Vistula, where he was the *shohet,* the ritual slaughterer, and where my grandfather Pinhas Menahem Singer was the rabbi and where the rabbi's daughter Hindele was not yet my mama, only a little girl. Since she has become a grass widow, and I suppose that makes me a grass orphan, we are Mr. Yakobovich's rent-free tenants in a first-floor room with a glass-encased balcony overlooking the back garden.

When Mr. Yakobovich left the shtetl for Antwerp to make his fortune in diamonds, he didn't take off his black caftan nor trim a single hair of his black beard, which is spread in splendor over his chest, nor tuck his sidelocks behind his ears. That, says Mama, is what other Jews do, bending over backward to please both God and the people over here. So to this day, now in Hatton Garden, he has remained a mere *mekler*, a broker. And on Friday mornings to make ends meet he becomes again a ritual slaughterer.

I post myself behind Mr. Yakobovich in the bare back room where he stands at a bench facing the window. Out shoots his left hand to extract live poultry, usually a chicken, from the shopping bag presented by housewife after housewife. Feathers fly, plucked from the neck by his right hand, which then picks up a knife. I sidestep to see a flash from the steel blade. And down plonks the bird, dribbling blood from its slit throat into an ever-wider pool of crimson.

I know that the hen is dead, but the hen doesn't know it, any more than it knows it won't be kosher before it's soaked in water and drained of every last drop of its blood. The swelling bulge of each tight-shut eyeball tells of a mighty struggle to reopen and see the light again. I also know I'll have forgotten the plucked feathers and the dribbling blood and the tight-shut eyeballs a few hours later when chicken soup is served at the Yakobovich table, festive with candles blessed for the Shabbas.

Before the first dish of gefilte fish, Mr. Yakobovich will stand erect at the head of the table, he's ever so tall, celebrating the kiddush over a glass of red wine. And his eyes will glower as dark—no, darker—than his jet-black beard. But this, says Mama, is because his love of the To-rah has been crossed. His two absent elder sons are gallivanting renegades. His twelve-year-old Jack rides a bicycle in the company of ruffians, and I know what Mr. Yakobovich doesn't know because Jack has told me not to tell anyone, and that is that he's going to be a Scotland Yard detective like the upstairs goy, Mr. Kaye, when he grows up. Mr. Yakobovich's only daughter, Rachel, is a chatterbox who laughs when she bends over to tickle me, and I look away from what I see inside her blouse. Whenever Mr. Yakobovich speaks to her, which isn't often, he looks away from her bare, plump arms. Mama says he can't wait to marry her off; the pity of it is she's only fifteen. Poor Mrs. Yakobovich does what she can to keep everybody happy. She's a lovely cook.

Mr. Yakobovich has never spoken a word to me, but he doesn't shoo me away on Friday mornings nor when I stand watching him brood over and poke at a tiny heap of blue-white diamonds. Our neighborhood has no Talmud Torah school, so he's arranged for me to take lessons with an out-of-work cantor from Antwerp. Mama, to pay the fee, has found work stringing colored beads into necklaces and bracelets.

7. DER DOPPEL-ZEKS

When Mama takes me to Der Doppel-Zeks for my first lesson, she explains it's not his real name, just a nickname given him at the Manchester Hotel, where, every time he won a game of dominoes with the double six, he joyfully yelled "Der doppel zeks!" But I must call him "Rebbe." He lives within easy walking distance but isn't much of a walker. "If the mountain of fat won't come to Moishele, Moishele will come to the mountain of fat," says Mama, laughing. Then in all earnestness she says she'll not come to fetch me if I promise by all that's holy to take very good care of myself, not to loiter nor speak to strangers on the way home. I promise.

Der Doppel-Zeks has no wife, no children. The stuffy attic he lives in is cluttered with books, and the air simmers with a meaty smell from the pot on the gas cooker. He sits on a wicker armchair and I on a low stool, wedged in between his belly and the door. I read the first word in the book open on my lap, "*B'reshith*," and he chants its Yiddish meaning, "In the beginning." To many a single Hebrew word there are several Yiddish words, and there's one word, "*ett*," to which there is no meaning at all. It's fun.

Every so often Der Doppel-Zeks's round little flushed face, framed with a curly, ginger beard, sinks onto his chest and his red lips bubble with a gentle snore. But even before he opens his kindly eyes he murmurs the Yiddish word or words that went missing when he fell asleep. If I mispronounce a word over and over again, he corrects me in his patient singsong over and over again.

Only once, a once I will never forget, he struggles to his feet, wobbly on his short legs, and shrieks at me, "*Hilul haShem!*" Thinking I'd got the word wrong I repeat it: "Yehovah." And he claps his hands to his ears, foaming at the mouth. When he comes to himself he tells me I've desecrated—I take that to mean shamed—Elohim's other name, which is too holy to be spoken. I'll not do that ever again. Instead of the unspeakable I'll say "Adonai," meaning My Lord.

Der Doppel-Zeks says the Rebboine-shel-Oilim, the Master of the World, will forgive an innocent child.

I come away well pleased with myself. I don't loiter, I don't speak to strangers, I keep my promise.

* * *

Der Doppel-Zeks is going away. A widow from Birmingham fell in love with his voice hearing him sing at a party in the house of a Hatton Garden merchant. She wants to marry him and set him up as the cantor in her synagogue.

I ought to be glad. Often enough, sitting with Der Doppel-Zeks, I wished myself far away from the smell of his stew. I was now able to read whole phrases, not only words, and I could easily have translated them into Yiddish, but he wouldn't hear of it. And he never, never skipped the boring lists of the names of the fathers and the sons, and the sons who became fathers, and how long they lived, hundreds of years.

But now that I'm at my last lesson I'm going to miss him. We had got to the story of the tower of Babel, and I do so want to know what will happen after Adonai scatters its builders to the far ends of the earth and splits their one language into a babble of languages.

On my way home I dawdle. Any time I hurt I'm good at pretending I don't hurt, but this once I don't want to pretend. I feel—I don't think—I feel bad about Adonai being unfair. He expects people, His own handiwork, to be perfect like Himself. Yet when they build the tower of Babel or do other things that will make them like Himself and his angels, He flies into a rage. If He didn't want Adam to eat the fruit of the tree of knowledge of good and evil, why plant it in the garden of Eden in the first place? Being Himself jealous, He should have known that Cain, whom He snubbed, would kill his brother Abel, whom He favored. What's more, why did He prefer the offering of slaughtered lambs to that of the fruits of the earth? And if Adonai hadn't put the rainbow up in the sky for a reminder not to bring on another flood, would He once again drown all his creatures save only the fishes?

It's raining—no rainbow over Clephane Road—and at the sight of a matchbox floating in the gutter I stop; I fancy I'm seeing Noah's ark. I'm being worse than naughty; I'm a sinner. I remember my daily Sh'ma Yisrael prayer: "Listen, Israel! Adonai our Elohim is the one and only God, and you shall love Adonai our Elohim with all your heart and with all your soul and with all your might . . ." I must and will love Him, though it's easier to love Elohim who in B'reshith blessed all his works than to love Adonai who, while saying that He himself was Elohim, went on to curse these same works.

I'm about to be punished. I don't look where I'm going. I trip on a loose flagstone, I fall into a puddle, and I lie there wet, my knees bruised, the palms of my outstretched hands stung. A gentleman—I know he's a gentleman because he wears a bowler hat and carries an umbrella—yanks me up by the scruff of the neck, replaces my skull-cap, which I'd forgotten to take off, and says, "Pain hurts, so have a good cry, little Jew boy!" I don't cry; I wasn't going to cry. I say "Thanks, mister!" and wish I hadn't.

8. ARMISTICE DAY

Jack, perched on a stepladder, unhooks the blackout curtains. Everybody except Mr. Yakobovich watches him. It's Armistice Day, or will be, starting eleven o'clock. "One meshuggaas is over," says Mama. Her wry laughter is a reminder of that other meshuggaas she laughs at once in a while, about her "Avrum who can be trusted to be in the wrong place at the right time." In Russia there's a Bolshevik revolution, and the czar for whom Papa was going to fight has been shot.

Back in our glass-encased balcony, where the Primus stove is a furnace close up and the chill all around is all the worse for it, Mama suddenly bursts into song. "*Lomer sih iberbeten*, let's make it up and be friends . . ." She drops the beads she's been stringing, puts on her fox stole, winds a woolen scarf round my neck, and we set off for Piccadilly Circus.

The bus stop we go to is crowded. Poppy-red omnibus after poppy-red omnibus spurting steam from its pug-nosed bonnet races past without stopping. These are singing buses. They rattle a drumbeat to "Take me back to dear old Blighty," "It's a long way to Tipperary," and other old songs bawled by the heads poking out of the lower-deck windows, by the people standing tightly packed on the open upper deck, by the men jamming the rear stairs. There are so many buses it's as if it's the one and same teasing bus going round and round the blocks of houses. Then along comes an omnibus that's different; it has the body of a man trailing from the bottom rear stair. Not to worry—his one hand clings to the rail and his other hand beats a tap-tap on the roadway to the roar in the chorus of "Rule Britannia!"

Daylight soon fades in November, and it's long since dark by the time we make it to the Circus. Daredevil climbers drape the statue of Eros— aloft is the one place where one can breathe. The crush below is like a saucepan on the boil. There's whooping and kissing and hugging. There's drinking from bottles and, once in a while, a splutter of vomit. There's singing to mouth organs and fiddles, to banjos and trumpets. There's dancing and changing of partners, young and old. Gentlemen in top hats dance with women in aprons. Working men in caps dance with ladies in furs. Among the dancing Tommies are some with empty sleeves; one dances with a cane in his hand—he's blind; another, one-legged, hops and skips with the help of a crutch. Mama is grabbed, and not by gentlemen. Tearing herself away, she stoops and shouts in my ear, "Meshuggaas!"

Back in Clephane Road I see the character who so often woke me up with his cries of "Take cover!"

Now armed with a long, flame-tipped pole he goes from lamppost to lamppost and lights the gas.

9. THE HOSPITAL

The pigeons on the roof of the balcony flap their wings and coo. Daisies in the back garden are waiting to be picked. I'm waiting for my bellyache to go away. I tinker with the Meccano set Mama bought me for my sixth birthday. The steel strips I try to build up into the designs printed on the lid fall to pieces. The plasticine shapes I mold are shapeless; I squash them. It's time I started school, only Mama doesn't want a Talmud Torah school, which is what Mr. Yakobovich wants. Der Doppel-Zeks is back from Birmingham, unmarried, but he now lives somewhere in the East End, the other side of town.

I slip upstairs hoping Mr. Kaye will be home. He's a lean and lanky redhead, and when I look up at his tiny, peaked face it's as if I'm seeing a bird perched on a telegraph pole, flown in from far away where strange things happen. Jack says he's a Scotland Yard detective and a Scotsman, and the woman he calls Mrs. Kaye, as tall as himself but plump, isn't really his wife, only his servant. He's strict with her and in a comic way pretends to be stern with me. When I don't eat the piece of cake she offers me, he knows I'm in pain and calls me a little rascal for not telling my mother.

Soon I don't have to tell Mama; I squirm, I can't help it. She takes me to the Metropolitan Hospital. After a long wait in the dingy green waiting room, a doctor examines me and says I'll be all right on three teaspoonfuls a day of the nasty medicine he prescribes. I'm not all right. The next day a different doctor prescribes a different medicine and says I'll be all right. I'm worse. Two doctors are joined by a third and he says I have acute appendicitis. I'm going to learn a lot of new long words.

Mama is sent away before she's done kissing me goodbye. I'm taken up in a lift, given a bath, and laid out naked on a glassy table in an all-white room. It's called the operating theater. I've not been in a theater before, which I always thought was something like the cinema where I've laughed at Charlie Chaplin and felt sorry for Mary Pickford. A white-coated doctor—all the doctors and nurses in the theater are white coated—clamps a mask over my face. It shuts out the dazzling white light. He tells me to breathe. I breathe what smells like the carbolic Mama uses for washing the floor. I go wooden.

I wake up in a ward for grown-ups. Two days later I'm again in pain. And again I breathe what I now know to be chloroform. When I wake up in the same bed, the scarlet scar down the right side of my belly has lengthened into a serpent with six pairs of legs, which are, in fact, stitches.

Mama says the surgeons are butchers. She has brought me a picture book. I take a particular fancy to the picture of a little girl followed by a lamb into a classroom full of laughing children. The old man in a dressing gown and slippers, who keeps shuffling back and forth in the aisle between the two long rows of beds, stops to look at it. He recites "Mary had a little lamb . . ." and teaches me to read. I then go on to "Jack and Jill went up the hill . . ." and other nursery rhymes, though Mary with the little lamb is still my favorite.

After a week or so, when Mama comes to fetch me, she says we're not going home to Clephane Road because the Yakoboviches are leaving for Antwerp. She has rented a room in a nice house with nice people near a nice park, but before moving in we're going for my convalescence to nice Southend-on-Sea. The trill in her voice expects me to be pleased, and I am pleased with new places to go to.

From her handbag—in it is a wad of pound notes, and she's not wearing her fox stole—she extracts a mousy-colored postcard for me to look at. The postage stamp is a mauve color like I've never seen before. And Mama is in a state like I've never seen before. It's as if all the miseries I've ever seen her in are mixed up with her happiness when she's telling stories of the *alte heim*. Is the postcard from Papa? No, it's from her mother and father, my Buba and Zeida.

On the way out I get a handshake from the old man in the dressing gown and slippers who taught me to read English.

10. SOUTHEND-ON-SEA

The train ride to Southend-on-Sea, rowdy with happy-go-lucky Cockney day-trippers, is all too short for my liking. Shouldn't the excitement of a new place be because it's a long way away? The seafront with its shingly beach does stretch away as far as the eye can see. So I have only myself to blame for a twinge of disappointment. I've come expecting to see smooth waters decorated with swans and sailing vessels, only real ones, not Finsbury Park toys.

Being a silly boy but of a happy disposition, soon enough I thrill with delight. Mighty wave after mighty wave crested with lacy white foam hurls itself in make-believe fury at the shore and playfully dribbles away. White seagulls swoop overhead. The promenade is loud with fun fair music and the cries of cockles-and-mussels vendors. At the far end of the long pier a steamer is ready to take me away to marvelous adventures in a far-off land.

A cloudburst sends everyone scurrying for shelter. Mama doesn't want to sit in the parlor of the kosher boardinghouse where the other guests play bridge and chatter in Yiddishy English. In our room she again shows me the mousy-colored postcard and sighs. "Your Buba, after all these years, having God knows how traced my address, couldn't be bothered to write her daughter a letter."

I look at the writing. The neat, straight lines are from Buba, leaving at the bottom only a small space for the flourish of blessings from Zeida. Buba tells of Zykow Stary, a Galician shtetl to which they fled from wartime Warsaw with young Moishele, after whom I'm named. Of my two other uncles, Yitzhak stayed behind while the eldest, Shiya, the Lord's mercy upon him, ran off to join the Bolsheviks in Russia.

With disdain Mama reads Buba's hope that Hindele and husband and child are well. Pleading a headache, she asks for lunch to be sent up.

And for the rest of the afternoon I am treated to a tale that, by means of repetition in the days and years to come, will linger in my mind as if inscribed on parchment.

The small Polish town of Bilgoray boasts of an orphan who is an *ilui*, a genius. Little is known of his parents, who perished in a typhus epidemic. When he, the nine-year-old prodigy, mounts the pulpit to deliver his first homily in the Great Synagogue of Lublin, the crush has Jews standing on each other's feet and hanging from the rafters.

At the first sproutings of a beard, the Bilgoray Hasidim implore him to become their zaddik, their saint who will hasten the advent of the Messiah. But he, Reb Mordehai, declares himself a misnagid, an adversary of the end of days cult and a believer in the Torah ruling that man shall return eternally to the dust out of which he was created.

Appointed rabbi of Bilgoray, he puts a trick question to delegates from Warsaw and other large cities come to lure him away to their congregations: "Do you have a *beth olim*, a cemetery in your town?" Reassured on this score, he turns the petitioners away with a shrug: "We also have one in Bilgoray."

A swarthy giant, there is to his presence an aura, which one Easter Sunday averts a pogrom. Standing on the porch of the synagogue, his impressive silence halts a mob of peasants come with hatchets and pitchforks to avenge the crucifixion of Jesus. They back off and disperse without bloodshed, without pillage, without rape.

Reb Mordechai's two sons are a disappointment to him. Both are ordained rabbis, but the one harbors grandiose mercantile dreams and the other is a dandy whose sidelocks and ritual fringes, when he gets excited, positively waltz.

On the other hand, he has a daughter Bathsheva worthy of him in learning and as dour a misnagid as he. She is a skeletal redhead with enormous gray-blue eyes in a gaunt face on a scrawny neck. With her he can engage in pilpul, the fine art of reconciling irreconcilables in Torah and Talmud.

Comes puberty, the time for marriage and motherhood. The choice falls on Pinhas Menahem Singer, in his teens already a Talmudist and Cabalist of the first order. His family tree reaches back through Yosef Caro, the medieval codifier of Jewish law and, it is said, to King David himself. Small and frail, with gentle blue eyes and a golden beard, he is a psalmist with no pretensions to the throne.

If ever a mismatch could be called perfect, Providence has contrived one. Pinhas Menahem is meek and submissive, which is what a wife should be. Bathsheva is stern and haughty, and were she the husband, nothing less would satisfy her than to be chief rabbi of Warsaw.

There is in the Singer family yet another mismatch between Pinhas Menahem's parents. His mother is the breadwinner. An itinerant dealer in antique jewels, she hobnobs with the Polish and Russian aristocracies, intercedes with the authorities when Jews are in trouble—but when are they not in trouble?—and, past the childbearing age, goes off to die in Jerusalem and be buried on the Mount of Olives. There she will be ready to spring to her feet the moment the Messiah shows up in Zion and blows the ram's horn. She well knows that all other Jews risen from their graves in the Galut, in exile, will have to crawl on their bellies to the Promised Land before they may at last hold their heads up.

The newlyweds are *kestkinder*, boarder children in the Bilgoray rabbi's household, till of an age to fend for themselves. For Pinhas Menahem to gain official recognition as a rabbi he must first pass the Russian-language exam required of the clergy in Poland under czarist law. Sent to Lublin to take private lessons, he plays truant and prefers to go singing and dancing at the court of the Ger Tsadik rabbi. With the millennium at hand, what need has he of a certificate delivered by goyim?

The years pass, dread years of sterility for Bathsheva. At last pregnant by the grace of God, she fully expects a son. As she considers that the Almighty has made a great mistake in creating her female, it is unthinkable that He would not seize this opportunity to make amends. But mysterious beyond understanding are His ways. Bathsheva's womb brings forth a daughter, to whom she refuses the breast.

In haste a wet nurse is found, whose generous nipples squirt milk all over the newborn's face. This good woman has a horde of children of her own to look after and a cobbler husband pounding away at his work in a one-room hovel. Where are they to put the crib of Hinde Esther, named after a great-grandmother who wore manly ritual fringes and went on pilgrimage to the Beltz Tzadik? Under the table; there is no other place.

Once a week, on the Sabbath eve, Bathsheva comes to look at—never to touch, let alone pick up and fondle—her misbegotten child. At the age of three, blinded by dust and cobwebs from the underside of the table, Hindele is brought home, and thanks to the benediction of the Bilgoray rabbi she recovers her sight. But for the rest of her life a glaze will blur her eyeballs and they will turn their gaze inward, toward what seems a monstrous, or at least a bewildering, apparition.

Is my mother endowed with a supernatural memory of her under-the-table outcast self and of things that happened before she was even born? Oh, no, she would hear of them in fine detail from her mother, Bathsheva. Storytelling runs in the family.

Pinhas Menahem too is a storyteller, but his are long, drawn-out tales of heavenly marvels and of miracles performed on earth by the thirty-six humble saints, artisans or even beggars whose identity no one knows and whose righteousness preserves sinful mankind from the fate of Sodom and Gomorrah. And when he tells these tales, his face is aglow with a modest sweetness that would truly befit one of these same thirty-six saints.

Bathsheva, a daylong reader of Hebrew and Aramaic esoteric books, sits on a couch with her tiny feet tucked under her and only occasionally looks up with a frown to reminisce about this and that in a few but well-chosen words. And in even fewer words she passes judgment on the follies and wickedness of various villains and fools regarded as wise and honest by their peers, who are no better than they are.

Following the birth of Shiya—a pet name for Yehoshua—two years after Hindele, the paterfamilias establishes himself as the illicit and ill-paid rabbi of Leoncin, as poor a shtetl as any in the *alte heim*. Six years later Yitzhak is born. Reb Pinhas Menahem is offered and accepts a post as head of a yeshiva, a Talmud academy under the patronage of the Radzmym Tsadik, who neglects to pay him his wages. So the family then moves once more, this time to Warsaw, to Krochmalna Street, the high street of an all-Jewish slum. There from morning till late at night the still-illicit, still-hard-up rabbi provides spiritual sustenance to the paupers who come to him with their woes.

Shiya and Yitzhak are alike in their mastery of Torah and Talmud but not in looks. Shiya, except for his fair hair and blue eyes, is the sturdy image of his grandfather Reb Mordehai. Yitzhak takes after his mother; he has her wraithlike presence, all skin and bones, deathly pale and freckled, with enormous gray-blue eyes, thin lips, sharp nose, and large, outstanding ears, which often flush a fiery red like his dangling sidelocks.

Bathsheva's favorite is Shiya. Hindele adores him but cares enough for Yitzhak to be evasive and not, as is her way, blurt out what she really thinks when he asks her, "Am I ugly?" For the rest, she doesn't know what to make of him. He hardly ever speaks. His forte is listening. He listens to her, who is given to fits of melancholy and ecstasy. He listens to Shiya, who dismisses religion as outworn superstition. He listens to the precocious prattle of beautiful Moishele born on Krochmalna Street. He listens to his father and the incessant stream of wretched callers. And he listens to his mother, Bathsheva (whose name with a masculine twist will eventually figure in his quasi-pseudonym Isaac Bashevis Singer).

Taciturn at home, Yitzhak allows himself to be drawn out by the downstairs grocer, who informs Hindele: "That lad has more wisdom in his little finger than the rest of us put together. Mark my word, one day the world will sit at his feet."

Hindele, the household drudge, devours Yiddish fiction and poetry. She has only one friend, a simple, good-hearted girl named Leicha. Once in a while she goes to see Yiddish plays acted by exuberant tragedians and comedians. Dressed in her long, best gown, befitting a rabbi's daughter, she also takes strolls in Warsaw's elegant Saxony Gardens. There, one day, she encounters a noble, emancipated, clean-shaven Jew who wears a cape and is a poet. They often talk with one another, but she cannot pluck up the courage for intimacy nor tell him that she writes short stories. She does, however, show her stories to Bathsheva, who reads them with raised eyebrows and without comment.

At twenty, Hindele without a dowry seems destined to remain a spinster. But Providence decrees otherwise. A preacher famed throughout Poland in the person of pot-bellied Reb Gedalya Kreitman—who raises huge funds for the Agudas Yisrael, guardians of ultra-Orthodoxy on a formal fifty-fifty sharing basis—comes to consult Reb Pinhas Menahem on a knotty matter of halakha. His eye is caught by the young girl who serves the lemon tea. She may or may not appear to him quite as sweet as the cube of sugar through which he sucks his tea, but he's well aware of her illustrious lineage. On the spot he proposes marriage—no, not to himself, who has a wife and all too many daughters still unwed, but to Avrum or Avraham, the most commendable of his three sons in Antwerp.

Reb Gedalya, of course, makes the offer only after the young lady has closed the door behind her. Bathsheva is called in and a match is arranged. She informs Hindele, who says, "You wish to see the back of me? Very well, I shall go into exile."

Whenever Reb Gedalya is in town, he calls on his son's betrothed and engages her in erudite conversation, for she is well versed in overheard pilpul, and before taking his leave, he drops on the table a "little gift" of fine jewelry.

On the train out of Warsaw, Bathsheva murmurs her apprehension that czarist inspectors may sniff sedition in the Yiddish script of Hindele's stories. Hindele hands over her several exercise books. Bathsheva tears them up and flings the shreds out of the carriage window.

In Berlin, Hindele and Avrum meet, stand looking at each other, and are sent off on a stroll, unescorted.

Before the bride takes her place under the wedding canopy in a kosher hotel, she lends a dutiful ear to a whisper from her father: "Do not be shy with your husband. What he and you will be doing is ordained by the Torah. It's a holy act of which your mother cannot have enough; she wears me out night after night."

This and much else that I hear from Mama Hindele in our very own kosher hotel is way beyond my comprehension. But I come away from Southend-on-Sea with the evanescent tang of cockles and mussels in my nostrils and with a persistent string of word-pictures that will hover before my eyes for the rest of my life and which by dint of repetition will gain coherence so as to become wholly intelligible.

11. PETHERTON ROAD

Home sweet home is a newly whitewashed attic in a tall house over a dairy on Petherton Road. I wake up to the clang and clatter of the milk churns on the pavement. And when I sit up in bed I don't bang my head because the pillow is where it should be, below the higher end of the ceiling.

On Wednesdays, in the small hours of Thursday really, my mother in her bed and I in mine are treated to a musical awakening. In the next-door attic the jazz-band leader from the Savoy Hotel holds rehearsals of what his mother, the dairywoman Mrs. Brooks, says are his own compositions. Each piece, after a brisk start headed for wherever it's going, stops short as if frightened, then turns back, then goes forward again only to lose its way once more. This goes on and on, the quarrelsome instruments desperate but also wonderstruck by the unexpected places through which they pass. In the years to come I'll dream dreams like that that will take me to splendid strange places where I'll get lost and find myself ending up nowhere.

After a disturbed night my mother goes back to her daily work, embroidering on silk blouses the flowers that pay for the rent and our keep. Wearing pince-nez, she sits at the narrow window through which in fine weather a shaft of sunshine spotted with dancing particles makes its misty way from ceiling to floor.

The narrow window looks out on to the sky. I have to lean over to see what lies below—a gravel roadway with the opposite row of houses many a stone's throw away. All in all, this small attic cluttered with the furniture from Clephane Road is better than cozy. It's home up in the sky.

There is to Petherton Road an out-of-town feeling. Along with the dairy, its only shops at the far end where it runs into Green Lanes are a draper's, a barber's, and a shop long since closed down.

I, Morris—no longer Moishele—run the errands for my mother. In the dairy I speak English with Mrs. Brooks, who knows no Yiddish. And she laughs at everything I say. A tiny woman, perched on a high stool behind the counter, she even keeps other customers waiting to have her laugh with me.

When my mother sends me off to deliver a bundle of embroidered blouses, which I carry like a baby in my arms, she makes me promise faithfully not to get myself run over in the Green Lanes traffic. I'm good at dashing across between two oncoming trams furiously tinkling their bells at me, and then I turn into Burma Road.

The half-dark of the back room where big-bosomed Mrs. Moses sits at a table drawing pencil patterns of flowers is thick with a *jene velt*, an otherworldly hush, because of Mr. Moses. No bigger than myself but with a white beard, he sits at a desk writing fast, very fast, pages for the Last Judgment, I suppose. The hush isn't even broken when Mrs. Moses sends me away with good health wishes for my mother and with the penciled silk blouses.

I'll soon be going to school, and I'm impatient for the start of the autumn term. Meanwhile I keep myself busy. I attend a Sunday Talmud Torah where Abraham is about to sacrifice his beloved Isaac. I've begun reading *David Copperfield*. I go to Clissold Park to look at the birds and the animals in the cages. I wait for the late-afternoon homecoming of our neighbor Mr. Brown the policeman, who calls me a young scamp and in the doorway takes off his helmet for me to look at—he knows that's what I want; it looks like the spiked belfry in a picture book. On some Fridays my mother takes me to The Lane in the East End, the liveliest market in London if not in the whole wide world. On the Sabbath we go across the road visiting Mrs. Ziegler, the sad but pleasant widow from Antwerp, who has a beautiful, shy daughter, Rosie, and whose twelve-year-old Jules is sure to grow up into a second Mr. Moses.

My mother has bought me a violin. She has read something in her Yiddish newspaper about a Jewish child prodigy at the Albert Hall. I take lessons. When I draw the bow over the strings it whines, it screeches, it's in agony. It has the fine color and gloss of the coffin I often stop to look at in the Green Lanes undertaker's shopwindow. Without it, my life on Petherton Road could be sheer bliss.

12. SCHOOL

My mother sees me to the boys' entrance of the Newington Green Elementary School. I find my way to the beginners' class and wait to be shown where to sit on one of the five long benches lined up in front of equally long desks. The other boys just scramble for places. I end up on the back bench.

The nine o'clock bell rings. The teacher, standing on a dais, a thin man with a gaunt face topped by glossy black hair, raps a ruler on his desk. He says, "I am Mr. Baker. You will answer 'Present, Sir' and raise your hand when I call the register."

He rattles off name after name. He stops short, smiling a thin-lipped smile. "What have we here, another member of the chosen race?" In a falsetto he reads "Mozes . . . Krajt . . . mana." He pauses, resumes his thin-lipped smile, and snaps "Yid, absent!" Only then do I remember to raise my hand. And I forget to lower it amid the burst of titters, all eyes turned toward me.

Done calling the register Mr. Baker has the class repeat after him the Lord's Prayer. I keep my mouth shut and store away new phrases—"kingdom come," "daily bread"—and new words—"hallowed," "trespass."

Mr. Baker turns to the blackboard on the wall and chalks up the first three letters of the alphabet. I sit through the lesson in a haze.

The bell rings. I follow my classmates into the playground. There they crowd me, yelling in chorus: "Yid, go home!" A boy much bigger than the others lunges out. I go sprawling on the asphalt. He stands over me, growling, "Coom on, git up an' put 'em up, you filthy Yid!" I look away from his knobbly knees, from his clenched fists, from his snarl, from his tousled flaxen hair, toward the thin-lipped smile on Mr. Baker's face. I pick myself up and again he knocks me down. Again I see Mr. Baker's thin-lipped smile. When the bell rings I pick myself up and am the last boy back in the classroom.

The noonday bell rings. I hurry out into Newington Green. My mother is waiting for me. She hasn't yet caught sight of me in the rowdy throng. She is smiling that same eager and wan smile as when she rejoiced because I would be going to school and she never had that good fortune. I come forward. Her eyebrows twitch, her eyelids flutter. Before she can ask questions I say, "Mama, I fell down in the playground."

She dusts me off. She takes me by the hand to the tram stop. Over lunch, every bite of which I eat though I'm not hungry, I say, "You were the only mother waiting for me to come out of school. They're going to take me for a weakling." She lets me walk back alone in good time for the two o'clock bell and for two more hours of haziness.

In playtime I make myself scarce, dodging and dashing around. The day after, the bully catches up with me. I put up my fists and get in a couple of punches before he has me down on the ground and kicks me hard. Again I lie waiting for the bell to ring and again I see Mr. Baker's thin-lipped smile.

After school I hang around outside the gate. I want to see more of Mr. Baker. Out he comes, a forward-leaning, dark figure striding off at a pace that has the kids at his coattails on the run to keep up with him. I too follow, intent on memorizing the image of this shadowy Satan with his retinue of doting little demons.

On the morrow and the day after I again put up my fists. But on the Friday the bully finds me in the urinal, where I stand along with other kids pissing against the wall. Before I can button up he has pissed on me.

I'm still wet when I get home. I tell my mother. She takes off my clothes, drops them into a basin of water, gives me a soapy bath in the downstairs bathroom, and on Monday morning takes me to school.

Under her glare, the janitor shrugs and leads the way through dim corridors to the headmaster's room. Before knocking on the door he cautions my mother to behave like a lady, because Mr. Raby is a country squire doing his Christian duty to a scruffy lot of monkeys who'd be better off with a helluva lot more caning.

Mr. Raby rises from his desk, bows slightly, and bids my mother take a seat. She returns his bow and remains standing. Not a muscle stirs on his rosy face topped by a fine mop of white hair as he listens to her Yiddishy English. She explains that she was asked by the teacher who enrolled me to show my birth certificate from Antwerp, which names me as Mozes Krajtmana, but she made quite sure to have me properly registered as Morris Kreitman. She twists her face into a would-be imitation of Mr. Baker's smile. And her voice hardens into a suppressed scream when she tells how I was "pished" upon.

Mr. Raby says, "Madam, you have done well to come and see me. No, do not leave before we have attended to this deplorable incident." He presses a button on his desk and orders the janitor to summon Mr. Baker.

I turn my head toward the door. It stays closed. But here stands Mr. Baker, a respectfully inclined, shadowy figure, to which the headmaster recapitulates in hearty English my mother's Yiddishy tale of woe.

A silence follows. The shadow speaks up softly, soothingly. "The name entered on the register was a clerical error; most regrettable. The culprit Lewis is, no, I'd rather not say mentally retarded, but he is a dunce now in my class the third year running. Whether or not he can be taught to read and write I don't know, but I shall teach him better manners. Of that, sir, you may rest assured."

The headmaster: "Whatever the case, there must be no more verbal or physical abuse. No, don't go yet, Mr. Baker. You will first tender your apologies to Madam and to her son."

"I offer my humble apologies," says the unsmiling shadow and is gone as it came, through the closed door.

I have witnessed the first of the many trials I shall attend during my lifetime.

13. GROWING UP

I spend my pocket money on the comics and on the boys' magazines telling how the sons of princes and lords in their public schools make mischief and take thrashings on bare bottoms without a whimper. Much as I envy them, I know my place, which is at the Newington Green school, where I've reached the third class without ever once having to hold my hand out for a caning.

The books I now read come from the shelf in the next-door attic. Mrs. Brooks says I may help myself to her son's old books. Her son who still holds Wednesday night jazz rehearsals. After *Gulliver's Travels* I go for

Dickens, not *Oliver Twist* with Fagin but *David Copperfield* with Mr. Micawber. He's real, not make-believe. And I'm on the lookout for more of his kind on my walks through London Town, which I've learned to love, though it's nothing like the *alte heim* of my mother's tales . . .

She, ever her lonely self, has made friends with a scarlet-faced, slit-eyed woman Leah, a dressmaker from Antwerp whose husband has gone missing in Russia like my father Avrum. Leah lives at the further end of Petherton Road with a daughter Helen, and when I see the two together it's as if I'm looking at a fat cat with her wisp of a kitten.

My mother expects me to act the big brother to Helen, who's a year older than myself and a liar, forever telling spiteful, big secrets. Because I listen and only nod, she takes me for a simpleton. That's one thing of which she makes no secret.

One Wednesday my mother decides to go and see a Yiddish play with Leah at the Pavillion Theatre in the East End. Helen stamps her little foot in a tantrum, afraid of being left all alone in the dark. Our two mothers put their heads together and decide to leave me with Helen.

In a large room with lace-curtained windows on the first floor I find myself in bed with Helen. Well, not exactly—in fact there are two bedsteads set tight together with separate bedclothes. The ceiling reflects the light from a lamppost. I try to think of something that will help me go to sleep. But somehow my head is empty.

After a while Helen speaks up in her shrill secret voice. "Let's go for a journey." When she slithers under her quilt I follow under mine. Her hand touches me. My hand reaches out to touch her. I move in with her. I mount her. I quake. She quakes. In a fierce embrace—no kissing, no petting—together we quake. Done quaking, I dismount, edge off onto my mattress, and slither back onto my pillow. I turn my head and see she's back on her pillow. We do not speak.

I now have something to think about—the unsuspected pleasure of my compulsive quakings. I've never felt anything like it. The kids at school call it fuckin' and tell of pokin' it up her cunt. Nothing of the sort has happened. I'm neither sorry nor glad. I'm sleepy. The next thing I know, the lace-curtained windows are bright with daylight.

When our two mothers who slept in the attic bustle in, Helen and I are dressed and she has already made the beds. Over breakfast, listening to my mother, I feel as if I'm seeing the whole Yiddish play performed to bursts of laughter and fits of sniveling in the audience. In an aside she whispers, "Morris, you haven't missed much. If only you could see *The Dybbuk* as I saw it played in Warsaw."

She has no idea of how I spent the night. It's odd the way grown-ups forget how they themselves started out as children. I promise my-self—at the age of nine neither a child nor yet a grown-up, and I've still a lot to learn—to try and remember.

Next week and the week after, our mothers go to see two new shows at the Pavillion Theatre, the one a tragedy, the other a musical comedy with Hasidic dances. And again in the same two-in-one bed Helen and I go on a journey.

At the third breakfast, with my mother warbling Hasidic tunes, sud-denly Helen leaves the table, thrusts her forefingers in and out of her ears, changes into one of her many frilly dresses—Leah's handi-work—and runs off.

I also run downstairs. Out in the street Helen stands earnestly talking to girlfriends older than herself. This once, leaning against a lamp-post, I look her over, which I've never properly done before. I like her skinny legs. I like the pink of her dress. I like the freckles on her little hollow-cheeked face. I like her reddish hair aglow in the sunshine. And I dislike her the same as ever.

Before I can look away Helen has spotted me. With that big secret tilt to her head she says something that brings on a chorus of giggles. Her friends turn and stare at me, stare hard. I feel their mockery behind me as I walk past.

I make my mind up never ever again to go on a journey with a girl I don't like, really truly like.

14. YOM KIPPUR

For the Yom Kippur fast my mother puts on a long dark dress. I've never seen her in it before; it could be the gown she wore for her wedding photo in Berlin. She lights a *ner tamid*—long-lasting—candle. Its wax fills only half a tumbler so that the flame of the tiny wick won't be snuffed out by a gust of wind.

My mother lays the table with an abundance of food for me—I'll not fast before I've had my bar mitzvah—and she helps herself to morsels in a silence that gives me the creeps.

When she picks up a prayer book and puts on a hat, I want to go with her to the Green Lanes synagogue, where—this I've heard from Mrs. Brooks—an opera singer turned cantor will sing. My mother says he's a *ba'al tshuva*—a penitent who'll conduct Kol Nidre, a prayer in which people swear to give up their wicked thoughts. Smiling, she tells me to wait till I'm old enough to have wicked thoughts. I ought to but don't tell her what wicked thoughts I already have.

After she's gone I could light the gas lamp to read, but instead of a dip into *Robinson Crusoe* I engage in a Kol Nidre of my own making. Past midnight, still no mother, and I go to bed. In a dream I hear a gruesome gargle. Opening my eyes I see in the faint glimmer of the candle my mother lying on her back in bed. Foaming at the mouth, she quakes from head to foot.

I must get the Browns or the Brookses to call a doctor; I'm afraid she's dying. But before I get to the door she's breathing quietly and is fast asleep. Shall I, shan't I wake her? A long, long time I stand over her and then go back to bed.

In daylight my mother, prayer book in hand and wearing her hat, stands by my bed. "After breakfast come and join me if you feel like it," she says and is gone.

Shall I, shan't I eat? I treat myself to one of the two hard-boiled eggs and a cold cup of cocoa. Then I put on a skullcap and go off to the Green Lanes synagogue.

I don't want to join my mother in the women's gallery. At the men's entrance the beadle stops me and asks, "Has your father given you a ticket?" "My father," I say, "is in Russia." He shoos me away.

I mean to get the better of him. Pale, hungry, and thirsty worshippers wearing their prayer shawls come out for a breath of fresh air. Mingling with them when they go back, I sneak past the beadle. Inside the synagogue I plump myself on a bench, on a pilfered seat. The opera singer-cantor does have a fine voice. A bearded man with sidelocks asks, "Can you read?" Reassured, he hands me an open prayer book, points to a prayer, and I read words I don't understand. I follow him when he goes out for a breath of air and try to reenter with him. The beadle pushes me away. I take a vow never to set foot in a synagogue again. I get up to go home. But I turn back. Entrance to the women's gallery is free.

I post myself behind the rear topmost bench where my mother won't see me. Perhaps if I go on looking at her bowed head long enough I'll know what I'm looking for. I give up and take a seat beside her.

This will not be my last Yom Kippur in a synagogue with my mother. There will be many others. For all that, I shall grow into a Torah-loving agnostic, and I will fancy I know what I was looking for and could not find after my squabble with the guardian of the Green Lanes synagogue.

15. THE HOMECOMING

I open the door and see my mother has a visitor seated over a glass of lemon tea and a plate of cream crackers at the little round table. I also see on my mother's bed his heavy overcoat and a peculiar fur hat. "Papa!" I shout and fling myself upon him before he can open his arms. Nestling against him I breathe in an unusual scent; I am with him in Russia. I raise my head, receive a prickly kiss on my cheek, and I get up and back away so he can look at his son grown into a schoolboy and see the satchel I dropped on the floor.

The faintly reddish growth of beard on my father's smiling face excites me; it tells of the hundreds, the thousands, the millions of miles he has journeyed to reach our attic on Petherton Road. And I behold promise of more excitement in the smile—no, not in his eyes anymore but in the tiny wrinkles puckered at the corners of his eyes. Wrapped in those smiling sprigs are the adventures he has had, the wonders he has known ever since that parting kiss—I haven't forgotten it—he gave me in Henry Road.

I perch myself on the edge of the bed beside my father's Russian fur hat and wait to hear exciting things. I well remember that he is no storyteller, but I expect my mother to draw him out. She sits unblinking for once, and silent. When his glass is empty she refills it. Then she sends me down to the dairy for a dozen eggs, butter, cheese, sardines, and yogurt on credit, and if I'm shy of asking the favor of a loaf of bread and if Mrs. Brooks can't spare one, I must go to the baker's in

Green Lanes. I ask for money; I will go to the baker's.

Rain has started pattering on the roof. My mother turns with a wan smile to my father. "You're going to miss the snow."

He shakes his head. "Not much snow in Odessa, and in the summer blistering heat."

On my return, my mother fries a huge omelet. My father eats slowly, very slowly, not to show how hungry, how very hungry, he is. When he's done eating my mother shrugs as if to shake off a spell of absent-mindedness.

She asks, "Has Yankele come back with you?"

He answers, "Yankele stays in Odessa."

"And Laiser?"

"Laiser is back with me."

"You mean there's no more *brogez*—you've made it up with him?"

He nods.

"Any news of your parents and your sisters? I have a weekly postcard from my mother and my father; they're in Galicia."

"My father Reb Gedalya is in Odessa."

"He followed his sons to Odessa?"

"No, he came not knowing we were there. When he ran away from Warsaw he chose Odessa for its Orthodox community. He came with a bag full of golden rubles, which the Bolsheviks took away from him."

"And you, Avrum, what did you do for a living in Odessa?"

"I did what I was ordered to do. I served notice on the rich to clear out of their homes."

"Did they offer you champagne? What will you have now, tea or coffee?"

"Either."

"And you, Morris, milk or cocoa?"

"Cocoa, please."

There are no more questions and answers. Such as they are they implant themselves in me like prickly seeds burgeoning into fantasies fertilized by the smiles at the corner of my father's eyes.

I lie awake not wanting to listen to my father's snores nor see in the dark the darkness of my mother still sitting up at the little round table. I hear again her question, "Has Yankele come back with you?" And in his answer and the smile that accompanies it—"Yankele stays in Odessa"—I hear the echo of the answer I gave my mother not so long ago: "I fell in the playground," not telling her how. Nor does my father tell—this fantasy straightway asserts itself into a certainty—that Yankele is dead. Which brings on the further certainty that only after the death of his twin brother did my father make it up with his elder brother Laiser.

I see again the ever so slight swellings to the folds in his smile as he tells of his father's bag of golden rubles being taken away by the Bolsheviks. Those swellings do not hide his glee. My curiosity is whetted by the spriglets round his eyes when he tells of doing what he was ordered to do, serving notice on the rich to clear out of their homes. I hope my mother will yet ask many, many more questions and get him to tell, if not everything, at least something of what lurks hidden within his smiling wrinkles.

In that hope I fall asleep.

16. BERESFORD ROAD

My mother says our attic is a cell in which the tallest of its three in- mates bumps his head on the ceiling, and the time is come for him to do something more useful. Wanted is a home of our own, and she rents a flat in Beresford Road. To furnish it—there's no more shelter to turn to, we aren't refugees anymore—she sells her pearls to an old friend of the Yakoboviches. He cheats her out of a fair price but does so, she says, with mercy. The other jewelers she first tried wanted the necklace for a song.

The ground-floor flat we move into is like the one in Henry Road only darker, much darker, or so it seems to me. For the front room, which is to serve as a parlor, the floor is laid with linoleum on which an oval mahogany table is matched by four chairs and a pair of armchairs. There is also a divan on which I'll sleep at night wrapped in the War- saw eiderdowns. The two iron bedsteads, the little round table, and the wicker armchair from the attic are set on the bare floor of the back room. The kitchen has a table covered with a checkered blue-and- white oilcloth.

After the first down payment my mother pawns her fox stole and a diamond brooch. Finding the money to pay the monthly rent is a con- stant worry. My mother sits embroidering Mrs. Moses's silk blouses at the parlor window. The poor light, even with the curtains thrust aside, is a strain on her eyes. She cannot carry on much longer as the family breadwinner.

Heaven be praised for the end of the *brogez* between my father Avrum and his elder brother Laiser. Not that I like my newcomer uncle, a big hulking man with a scowl, which suits him far better than his grin. His fat wife I detest. The knowledge that his skinny but pretty daughter is my cousin horrifies me. It positively gives me the creeps. Never mind; Laiser has learned and passes on to his reconciled brother the skills of a framer of ladies' handbags. The furniture shop won't be sending a van to recover unpaid-for merchandise.

Christmas is coming. It's the busy season. An Antwerpener, Mr. Rose, whose factory cannot accommodate another worker, wants my father to frame ladies' handbags at home. Our kitchen table is stripped of its checkered blue-and-white oilcloth, and tools and a riveting block no different from a cobbler's are set up on it. My father hammers away at the iron frames called sheens. On these dull sheens he fastens and rivets the frames, glittering nickel or gilt casings befitting the fine leather ladies' handbags. From early morning till past midnight he's at it. No sooner is the cloth he uses to wipe the sweat from his face sopping wet than he drops it for a dry one.

Alfie, the weak-kneed delivery boy—he's a middle-aged man but has the slight build and the face of a witless child—is a daily out-of-breath caller with a cart to deliver unframed and collect framed handbags. He has to be talked into taking a rest on the edge of a chair. And my mother won't let him go before he's downed a cup of tea.

Christmas, more's the pity, comes but once a year—a year more often slack than busy. When slack my father draws the dole and is never at home between a breakfast of porridge and a supper of boiled potatoes and cabbage. When he's busy my mother leaves the house. Her eyesight has finally failed her for the embroidery of silk blouses. She,

Hindele, can't stand the *rat-tat-tat* of Avrum's hammer on the riveting block. It reminds her, she says, of her under-the-table self in a cobbler's hut way back in her ever-beloved *alte heim*.

She daily walks me home from school and has the grace to post herself not at the gate but on the other side of Newington Green—this after she gave up sitting in the little park where she was pestered by loungers littering the benches with empty beer bottles.

The unforeseen happens. It always does.

My mother waits for me in front of a greengrocery. It's a windowless shop shuttered at night. When open its fruit and vegetables are piled high on shelves, forming a sort of steep stairway. At its summit sits a woman, Mrs. Glaser, looking like an enormous flesh-and-blood replica of one of those dolls in the shape of an egg that, painted to resemble a grotesque human, will wobble at the flick of a child's finger as if about to tumble but will teasingly keep its balance. Her face, with the flush of an overripe tomato, has the slit eyes of the people among whom she grew up in faraway Russia, bordering on Manchuria.

Old-timers among Mrs. Glaser's rare customers have it that never once, in the past thirty or forty years since she was widowed or deserted by her husband—on this there are differences of opinion—has she spoken more than three or four words at a time to a living soul. So how is it that she holds long conversations in a foreign-sounding Yiddish with my mother? The long and the short of it is an offer from Mrs. Glaser, who owns the next-door house, to let the longtime-empty shop to my mother at a monthly rental of a measly few shillings. Not wishing to offend Mrs. Glaser, my mother promises to think the matter over. When she, the daughter of Reb Pinhas Menahem and Bathsheva, tells me about it she laughs herself into hysterics.

One evening my mother drops to the floor in the kitchen and lies on her back, writhing from head to foot and foaming at the mouth. I tell my father when he comes home for supper. "What, again a fit?" he says, and calls it the falling sickness. I now realize that what I saw on Kol Nidre night when she didn't fall but lay in bed was worse, much worse than a nightmare. He explains why he has kept her and me in the dark. It's because she doesn't know of her fits and because there's no cure for the falling sickness. Seeing me in shivers with fright, he promises to break the horrid secret.

On the morrow I take a day off from school. My mother wants her son, not her husband, to accompany her to the outpatients' department of the Metropolitan Hospital. A doctor hears her out and refers her to the National Hospital for Epilepsy in Bloomsbury. There she is accepted as an inpatient.

On Sunday I go visiting her in a large ward where women of all ages lie or sit up in the two face-to-face rows of beds. I bring her a book from the public library where, after Gorky, I've fallen in love with Tur-genev. My mother puts on her pince-nez, reads the title—*A Sports-man's Sketches*—and asks for Tolstoy's *Anna Karenina* next Sunday. She has little to say, and I can't think of anything better to talk about than the pranks of Pussy, the stray white cat who has adopted us in Beresford Road. When the visitors' time is up, I lower my head for a kiss and leave with a bad conscience.

I want to get lost. I go roaming all the way to the Houses of Parliament and the Thames Embankment through different streets and neighbor-hoods, each with a character of its own. On my way back, in Trafalgar Square, I gaze up at Nelson on his lofty pillar overlooking the mon-umental old cities, the slums, the new-built towns, and the straggly villages that all together make up London. While contemplating the statuesque admiral I think of Beresford Road and rickety Alfie, the de-livery boy, who'll not be in church, not on a busy Sunday. I hope that my father, Avrum, replacing Mama Hindele, will force him onto the edge of a chair and serve him a refreshing cup of tea. Turning away from Nelson I count the pennies in my pocket. Will they suffice for admission to the National Gallery of Art? This they do with twopence to spare. I enter and stop and start within inches of remote worlds peopled with strangers and longtime acquaintances, with merrymakers and mourners, with workers and idlers, with warriors and lovers, with the fully clothed and the wholly naked, with gods and goddesses. I both exult and feel sorry for myself at not having seen them in the flesh. I pause before the Rembrandts. This I do not only because of the magic of the name. I return to the *Self Portrait*, to the *Woman Taken in Adultery*, and to the *Jewish Merchant* because them I do see in the flesh and in mysterious light out of deep shade, the all-too-deep shade of real life.

My mother leaves the National Hospital for Epilepsy with pills that hopefully will stave off fits. Again when I come out of school she waits for me on the other side of Newington Green in front of the outdoor stairway of fruit and vegetables topped by Mrs. Glaser.

Blinking frenziedly, with a frightening smile, my mother says, "Never in my wildest dreams did I dream of . . . of guess what?" She, unlike myself, always remembers her dreams and often tells them to me. Now I hear, as if in a waking dream, that she has rented the next-door shop.

17. GROCERIES

My mother pursues the "wildest of her waking dreams" with subdued impatience and common sense. Alongside the greengrocery she will set up a general grocery store for the convenience of shoppers. Mrs. Glaser is well pleased with this arrangement. It's good for business, but more important it means personal companionship. She advances a loan for renovation of the dilapidated shop and for the installation of a counter and fixtures. An East End wholesaler is found willing to supply a modest stock of groceries on credit.

Not on the opening day but soon after my father puts in an appearance. He gives the shelves a glance and, with his back turned to my mother, posts himself motionless at the shopwindow. There he stands brooding a long while and departs as he entered, without a word or a nod.

This once I see no trace, no hint, of a smile at the corners of his eyes, let alone his lips. And this once, without really thinking about it, the haze is lifted from the way I feel about him. Feelings are that much plainer than thoughts. Unlike my Mama Hindele, who craves to belong and has done so from birth onward when denied her mother Bathsheva's breast, my Papa Avrum spurns all sense of belonging. For his comfort he stops short of acting the recluse. A diamond-cutter in Antwerp, it suited him to accept the despised golden rubles from his father Reb Gedalya, whom he hated. Needing the regular opportunity to go on a journey and quake at will, he accepted to travel to Berlin and marry a strange woman who bore him a son. In Odessa he took pleasure in evicting the rich from their mansions, not that he would throw his lot in with the Bolsheviks or any other party, movement, or creed. In Beresford Road, for a square meal he is ready to sweat past midnight framing ladies' handbags on the riveting block when business is busy. When it is slack, for boiled potatoes and cabbage he is not too proud to collect the dole. And his persistent smile fends off with covert malice the overt malice awaiting a declared outsider. This once he could afford to dispense with a smile for an unloved and unloving wife who, ever lonesome and ever boastful of her *yihus,* grand lineage, at last sits where she belongs, behind a counter selling groceries.

To my shame, I can't help feeling that I'm better off with a father who doesn't care for me than with a mother who cares too much for me. Mornings I escort my mother to her grocery and dash across the park to the school gate. In the two-hour lunch break I join her for the meat dish she has prepared overnight, which I heat up on the gas cooker in Mrs. Glaser's kitchen. While I'm about it I also stoke up the coal fire at which Mrs. Glaser's shriveled father sits slumped, as if dead.

After school I deliver to overdressed elderly ladies their lightweight purchases. They patronize my mother for her *alte heim* anecdotes. If only she wouldn't tinge her reminiscences with the *yihus* of the Singer family all would be well. Oh, how I wish my shortsighted mother could see as I see that sour-sweet blend of amused skepticism and heartfelt compassion on her customers' faces! Wishing is the most futile of exercises. These ladies coax me for information about my father, on whom they have never set eyes. I shrug as if I can't understand their fishwife Yiddish; I look askance at them when they talk to me in their halting English and shrink from the tip they try to thrust into the hand of the fairy-tale-spinning, grocery woman's nitwit son.

Every so often after school I collect heavy loads of sugar, butter, or other staples from the East End wholesaler, a skullcapped Jew. My efforts to make him speak to me in Yiddish remain unsuccessful. He has me sign a receipt and sends me packing.

At eight o'clock, closing time, my mother sighs over the day's takings. She goes early to bed. I lie on my divan immersed in Chekhov. He's less endearing than Turgenev, but his unhappy characters ring a bell in me. Stuck on the Russians, I'm wary of Tolstoy after having read somewhere something about his lovesick philosophy.

* * *

At school I half flunk the routine scholarship exam and am not sent to a secondary school where I'd be taught Latin. Instead I've started to learn French at Stoke Newington Central School. Bookkeeping, for which I've no use, is obligatory. An hour three times a week after the final bell, shorthand typing in an upper room with a Remington or Underwood typewriter on each desk is optional. I never miss that hour. The teacher, Mr. Cooke, a wisp of a man whose joviality verges on clowning, also gives history and geography lessons, which I mentally scrawl in Clarke's shorthand.

For English literature we have Mrs. Connell, a tall, gaunt woman with a falsetto voice. She picks on this or that boy to recite in turn so many lines from Shakespeare. It falls to my lot to have to speak Julius Caesar's dying words "Et tu, Brute? Then fall, Caesar!" She keeps me at it till I finally manage to come up with the tone of pathos and contempt befitting the treachery of the honorable man who has betrayed me. When we go on to *A Midsummer Night's Dream* I want to but cannot share Mrs. Connell's ravishment over the comedy's gems of wisdom and whimsy. There is in my twelve-year-old self an inborn Hasidic resentment of the Bard's scorn for sheer joie de vivre. Contrariwise, outright tragedy is my cup of tea.

In French with stern Mademoiselle Lebrun, whose only concession to her position as a Parisienne is the frilly white collar on her long black dress, we're past singing "Au clair de la lune" but still have a long way to go before we get to read Maupassant in the original.

I lose my one and only friend, George Revonitz, who, with brains to match his excess of fat, has made it to a secondary school. He still invites me home for Shabbas. His three pudgy sisters still look bemused at me—as if I were a goy eating strudel without saying grace after several helpings—when I swap *alte heim* tales in Yiddish with their stout mother. Their father, the baby-faced giant and master goldsmith, still pouts like the dumb character I once saw in a farce at the Pavillion Theatre. But no matter how much sugar I put into my lemon tea it tastes sour. It gets to be so sour I pay one last final visit.

On the following Saturday—and on many more Saturdays—I go rowing on the river Lea. More than a stream but hardly a river, the Lea flows between banks neither rural nor urban. I don't regret the money I spend on renting the rowboat.

Over long distances the drab scene keeps changing but remains ever dreamlike. It's like myself—an oddity.

18. THE LETTER

A parcel bearing a Polish postage stamp is waiting for my mother on the kitchen table when we come home from the shop. She examines it before opening the wrapper. There is to it the size and feel of a book. And a book it is, of Yiddish short stories: *Perl* (*Pearls*) by I. J. Singer. The flyleaf is autographed "To Hindele from Shiya." She puts on her pince-nez and, leaving her supper uneaten, retires to the bedroom now furnished with a wooden double bed.

On the morrow in the shop—and on many more morrows of which I lose count—she sits behind the counter reading her brother's stories. I expect her to tell me what they are about. I also expect to hear again how in Warsaw she also wrote short stories, which her mother Bathsheva tore to shreds and flung out of the carriage window in the train bound for the wedding in Berlin.

But my mother no longer voices her intimate thoughts in my presence as she used to do when she reckoned I was too young to understand what she was saying. Nor does she tell me what's in the fat envelope she wants me to send by registered mail. I see it's addressed to I. J. Singer, 32 Leszno Street, Warsaw.

On my return from the post office she asks me to look after the shop in her absence. She stays away a long time and comes back, out of breath, to inform me that she will soon be giving up the grocery. Mrs. Glaser did try to talk her out of it but ended up by saying "*Ge gezunterheit!*"—meaning "Go in good health!"

My mother still has fits. I was all along afraid she might one day be stricken in the shop. It never happened. But of the thousand and one reasons for my surge of relief at the prospect of quitting groceries, the one that counts above all else is being rid of that haunting fear.

I can guess what was in my mother's letter but not what Shiya's answer will be. Will he invite her to Warsaw? And if not, will she go uninvited?

My mother strikes a deal with the East End wholesaler. He will take back her unsold stock and refund half its cost. This will more than cover her outstanding debt to him. And she will remit the balance to Mrs. Glaser, who is ready to forgo part of the loan she advanced for the renovation of the shop, which of course remains her property.

The clearing out of the grocery store passes off peacefully. Meanwhile I lay hands on my uncle Shiya's book *Perl*. The title story runs to forty pages. It portrays a Jew in Warsaw bearing no resemblance whatsoever to any of the Jews in my mother's *alte heim* tales. He spends six wintry months in bed. Strapped to his skeletal chest is a bag heavy with pearls and diamonds. Tied to a string round his waist is a spittoon in which he meticulously collects the phlegm of a slight cough, part chuckle, part sigh, the while telling himself his lungs are gone, nothing is left of them. A moronic and epileptic nephew tends to his bodily needs in the dust-smothered, cobwebby six-room apartment, all windows shuttered in a five-storied tenement house, of which he is the landlord. Once in a while he gingerly steps out of bed to inspect the safe, where he keeps the rest of his hoard of jewelry.

Only when the summer heat is stifling and the sun tucks a mat of shadows under his footsteps does he put on his galoshes and a felt-lined, fur-trimmed overcoat and sally forth in a droshky to the cafés to meet young upstarts who like himself are dealers in precious stones but who unlike himself have never been to Amsterdam. They are bent on making their fortunes and wreaking misfortune on others. His next stop is the Saxony Gardens, where, seated on a bench, he scans the daily *Courier* for the large, black-framed death notices of fellow Amsterdammers. Well pleased to attend their funerals, he surveys his own monumental tombstone in the forefront of the cemetery. Engraved on it is his name, Moritz (Mendel) Shpielrein. Still to be filled in is the date of his demise, for which he is in no particular hurry. He still has business on hand, the completion of a sixth floor to his five-story tenement and the construction of a passage linking its court-yard to the one next door, which is also his property. First a widow and her guttersnipe children have to be thrown out of their single room, which is blocking the way. With the work in satisfactory prog-ress, Moritz Shpielrein plays a prank on a dear old acquaintance, the undertaker. He summons him on a false alarm to lay to rest the last of the Amsterdammers.

After *Perl*, Russia in turmoil is the setting of all the other short sto-ries. And short they are, presenting in staccato strokes the operations of revolutionary and counterrevolutionary forces in Kiev and Kon-stantingrad. Whatever their ideology, to which no reference is made, they appear indistinguishable in their one common purpose of mass slaughter.

My mother is on tenterhooks for a letter from Shiya. None is forthcom-ing for weeks and months on end. I have meanwhile elaborated two irrefutable arguments against the holding of a bar mitzvah celebra-tion for myself. The one, at the back of my mind and which I had far better keep to myself, is to the effect that Elohim, inscrutable creator of the universe, is best served by adoration of the gift of life, whereas Yehovah is not Elohim at all but an immortal human exacting worship from the mortals of the zoological garden he has created on earth. The other one at the tip of my tongue is a simple reminder that the Torah neither commands nor mentions the synagogue bar mitzvah ritual. I murmur it when my mother, having noticed the date on her Yiddish daily newspaper, cannot forgive her tearful absent-minded self for hav-ing overlooked my thirteenth birthday. Done hugging and kissing me, she rushes out to buy me a present. I ask for Chekhov's collected plays and tell her she's sure to find a copy of it in Foyle's bookshop.

When my mother no longer expects an answer from Shiya it turns up in the letter box. Brief and to the point, it invites his sister Hindele to spend the summer with him, his wife, and their two children in a dacha. A dacha, I suppose, is a holiday resort.

19. A SENTIMENTAL JOURNEY

"I beg you, Avrum, don't forget to feed Pussy!"

At the front door in Beresford Road, such are my mother's parting words to my father in the fond belief that this is the last she will ever see of him. He nods and smiles.

Suitcase in hand, I am at pains to believe that this pilgrimage with my mother back to her *alte heim* is really happening. However, reality asserts itself to the drumbeat of the Dover train, to the pitch of the Ostend-bound ferryboat, to the fumblings of my mother in her large handbag for our brand-new Polish passports, which are duly stamped by the customs official after having inspected them with an air of disdain.

Reality imposes itself when we board a local train to Antwerp. I cannot help the fact that I was born there, and I cannot restrain my mother from retracing in reverse her unforgivable journey into exile.

On arrival, we walk through streets familiar to my mother—she doesn't ask her way—streets lined with tall, tight-pressed houses that lean forward just enough for the ornate copings to gaze down in heady admiration at the pastel yellowish gray tint of their own facades.

We enter one such house, climb flights of carpeted stairs, ring the bell at a door boasting a large glossy mezuza—and my mother falls into the arms of Mrs. Yakobovich.

The apartment has two spare bedrooms. Jack, the once-upon-a-time aspiring Scotland Yard detective, is away in Brussels studying at a university. Rachel, who in Clephane Road was too young to be married off, is already an expectant mother. Mr. Yakobovich, with strands of white to his beard but with his caftan jet-black as ever, prospers as a dealer for a son-in-law whose diamonds are exclusively blue-white. Picture postcards on display in the souvenir shops show Antwerp to have a broad river Scheldt, a busy port, a cathedral with Rubens paintings, a palatial villa in which Rubens lived, museums with Rembrandts, and many, many other treasures. But I do no sightseeing.

If my memory serves me right, it is on Pelikaan Street that my mother lies astride the tram lines, stricken with the falling sickness. When she picks herself up, unaware of her fit, and finishes crossing the street, I make a vow that will determine the course of my life for all too many years. Come what may I'll remain at her side, acting as an unobtrusive guardian. Like the tram that stopped short of slicing through my mother and then, tinkling its bells, proceeded on its way, I carry on as if nothing inopportune had happened.

We leave Antwerp for Brussels. There I want to see something of the city, but my mother insists on hanging around in the railway station for a train that will deliver us to Warsaw at the prearranged hour.

I feast on the scenery gliding past the carriage window. Even when here and there it repeats itself, it does so in jazzlike variations to the nonstop thunder of the train. And there are interludes, halts in towns where our ever-crowded third-class compartment changes its passengers.

Flemish- and French-speaking Belgian families are followed by German laborers. My mother, who sits in a corner reading Heine's *Buch der Lieder*, tries her Hochdeutsch on them. Whether or not they understand what she is saying, they respond respectfully in what sounds to me like gibberish. Cheeks bulging, they munch enormous sandwiches and have the grace to look away when she extracts delicacies from the bag of provisions with which Mrs. Yakobovich saw us off.

Soon the carriage window offers nothing but a dim reflection of ourselves. It's going to be a long ride on a long train—the longer the better I tell myself as I go walking the length of the corridor. Underfoot, since it seems to me the wheels have become part of myself, a continent rolls away unseen. But I do see the people in the third-, second-, and first-class carriages and the several sleeping cars in which undressed ladies and gentlemen haven't bothered to draw the curtains. In this express train hurling forward through the night everyone is so close together and yet so far apart—*nu*, it's the same way the world over.

My mother falls asleep and I do not wake her when the train glides on a viaduct above the rooftops of Berlin, past dark Gothic spires, past domes set aglow in opal tints by the late afternoon sun. My curiosity about what goes on below in this summer of '26 all but smothers the queasy, lingering presence of a wedding canopy in a kosher hotel, by the grace of which here am I riding on a hotel on wheels.

Back on ground level the train picks up speed to a drumbeat of muffled thunder. Soon the window has nothing more to offer than the reflection of the dimly lit compartment. Sitting by my mother I go to sleep and dream disheveled dreams.

On the morrow the coach is loud with twittery Polish and with *alte heim* Yiddish. I take the suitcase down from the rack for a change of clothes—a Burma Road silk blouse with embroidered flowers for my mother and an open-necked white shirt for myself. I wait my turn to get into the men's lavatory. It's smelly, it's puddly, and I hurry to come away relieved, refreshed. My mother is a long time gone. She returns with a crimson streak of eager expectancy on her thin lips. But the black frizzy hair on either side of the chalk-white parting bristles with a forboding of disappointment.

20. A SUMMER IN SWIDER

The train pulls into the Warsaw railway terminal. I help my mother down three steep cast-iron stairs onto the platform and we join the crowd streaming to the exit.

"Look, Mama, isn't that Yitzhak over there?"

In a flash of illumination I recognize the deathly pale scraggly redhead with enormous gray-blue eyes, thin lips, and large ears who stands daydreaming beside the steam engine. He is her younger brother, the one who at dead of night climbed into bed with his sister Hindele. She, terrified of the evil spirits in the dark, enticed him with a temptation he couldn't resist—she'd tell him a story.

My mother gazes at grown-up Yitzhak in disbelief. He steps forward, darts at her two kisses, which miss either cheek, and strides away. We race after him to another railway station and board a dilapidated old train that chugs slowly out of town, stopping every few minutes to drop off sportily dressed passengers, commuters to dachas. We are left with black-caftaned Jews whose sidelocks and ritual fringes swing to the rhythm of their loud and plain Yiddish.

With the elusive Yitzhak my habitually overeffusive mother is at a loss for words.

We step out onto an open-air platform in the middle of nowhere. A signpost says SWIDER. We walk on burning-hot sand that smothers our feet and enter a forest strewn with pinecones. The air is heady with pine sap and birdsong. The golden sun in the bluest sky I have ever seen spreads light and shade with the absoluteness peculiar to dreams. We enter a fenced-in pinewood estate, and here the waking dream takes an uncanny turn.

Yitzhak is no longer at our side but stands before us grown taller and older. The gaunt face has become handsome; the ears still stick out, but they no longer look like the wings of a bat about to take flight. The massive bulging cranium has lost its mop of red hair, the chin is upturned, stubborn, and most striking of all, the same pale blue eyes are opened wide, but the indifferent faraway gaze has given way to a strange light in the whites of the eyes, a glitter of absolute authority and absolute melancholy.

This is my other uncle, Joshua Singer, or Shiya. With a shriek of mingled joy and pain my mother throws herself upon him in an embrace so passionate as to be more than sisterly. He struggles to disengage himself, takes a backward step, and fixes her with a glare of mingled sorrow and revulsion.

My mother stands abashed. She blinks frenziedly, bites her lower lip smeared with lipstick, and takes manifest note of what her beloved brother leaves unsaid: "You, Hindele, have been invited to a family reunion out of pity, or call it compassion, but certainly not love. I won't have you thrust yourself upon me. You have already managed to make a pest of yourself, so the sooner you go back to your unloved husband in London the better."

For the rest of our stay she will hold herself aloof from Shiya, will look down on his wife Genya as unworthy of him, will ignore and be ignored by Yitzhak, will consort with the dacha literati, and have little to say to me. As of now her past is a closed book, and I have ceased to be her audience.

Swider is the summer dacha of the Yiddish writers and poets. The rented bungalows are scattered far and wide in the pinewoods. These clapboard structures are each composed of a spacious living room flanked on either side by a bedroom and a kitchen, the whole fronted by a veranda on stilts.

Shiya installs a camp bed for me in the family living room. I have no notion where and with whom he accommodates my mother. She joins us for meals, but for the rest spends her time in feverish debate with the writers of *mamaloshen* Yiddish prose and poetry.

With breakfast still a long way off, I go feasting on the outdoor fragrance of pine sap laden with birdsong. Barefoot I tread the golden sands, which in the noonday sun scorch my feet. I probe the hidden meaning of the pattern to the fallen pinecones. I discern all manner of hairy and furry creatures in the fragments of cloudless blue sky visible through the thicket of treetops. And after a tempestuous downfall of rain, I wade high in waterlogged wheel ruts above a second sky mirrored underfoot.

The well-established daily routine is sometimes prone to the unexpected. One morning at breakfast with milk still warm from the cow's udder, with a choice of delicious soft white cheeses spread on crusty, fresh-baked rolls, one of the literati walking past pauses and leans over the veranda balustrade to ask Yossele, Shiya's youngest son, what he wants to do when he grows up.

Seated on a cushion to raise his elbows to table level, Yossele ponders awhile and then says, "When I grow up I'll take Papa up on the roof and give him a whipping." Fair-haired and bony, he is bitterly jealous of his father's favorite, Yasha of the cherubic face and the pretty dark curls.

Another time Yitzhak cracks open a boiled egg, takes an awestruck sniff at its stench, and says, "Such, yes, such is life!" There is an instant of silence followed by a burst of hilarity that rocks the table. His meditative air, head bent over the bad egg, raises the mirth to a new pitch. Even melancholic Shiya grins. My mother, only half amused, echoes, "Such, yes, such is life!" My aunt, dumpy Genya, very nearly tumbles off her chair laughing. Recovering herself, she says, "He has a way with him that is unnatural!" A fresh egg is served and breakfast is resumed in a subdued mood.

There are no other children of my age; I have to entertain myself. I take up a new form of sport: uncle watching, and it seems to have many other practitioners. The dacha hums with talk of the relationship between the two Singer brothers.

I am cast in the role of the legendary *haroeh v'lo nireh,* the heaven-sent carnal phantom who sees but cannot be seen by others. This arrangement is heaven on earth for me.

Every day my aunt Genya has me take time off from seeing without being seen to go and summon my two uncles to lunch. First I set out in search of Yitzhak. He spends his mornings perched somewhere or other on a pine tree, and part of the fun is locating the particular tree. In lofty seclusion he reads Yiddish, Hebrew, Polish, and German fiction and rereads Spinoza and Kant. How do I know, since he never talks to me? I hear it from the literati who are waiting for him to descend and favor them with one of his impersonations. When he chooses to perform, so they say, there is not a clown in the length and breadth of Poland who can hold a candle to my uncle Yitzhak.

He proves deaf to my call—his way of telling me to come again. I run off to fetch my other uncle. He too is up in the air. In the attic of a disused bungalow beneath a broken roof on which birds nest my uncle Shiya is busy writing. He sits on a stool before a bare wooden shelf that serves as his desk. Bemused, I watch his pen glide over a foolscap sheet, forming line after line of graceful script with never a pause. On second thoughts he does every now and then return to an earlier sheet, instantly locating the line where he changes, adds, or deletes a word. I stand behind his back, respectfully waiting for him to put down his pen so as to deliver my invitation to come for lunch.

He never speaks to me, yet one day the silence is broken, and he swings round to ask: "In what language do you think? Yiddish or English?" I think and think and answer truthfully: "Neither Yiddish nor

English." The melancholy in the whites of my uncle's light-blue eyes flashes suspicion: Is this chutzpah, a show of disdain to avenge my mother, or am I just an honest imbecile? He resumes his writing and will never speak to me again.

If only he had not turned away so impetuously, I might have had a chance to collect my wits and say simply that when I am happy I do not think in words. And, oh, how happy I am in this summer in this forest, in his company—too happy to take offense or even to feel sorry for my mother. Ever since I set foot in Swider I have been busy reaping a harvest of impressions too rich to be ground into verbal flour or kneaded and baked into the bread of common sense.

I return to where my other uncle is up a tree—in more senses than one. The way the literati phrase it—*er hengt inder luftn*, he hangs in midair. At twenty-two, under cover of a variety of pseudonyms—none yet Bashevis Singer—he dashes off kitsch romances for serialization in the local Yiddish dailies. He also publishes witty interviews and writes merciless book reviews. He has translated Thomas Mann's *The Magic Mountain* into Yiddish. All this is paid peanuts but is sufficient for his frugal needs. He doesn't smoke, doesn't drink, is a vegeterian; in fact he scarcely eats at all.

The literati at the foot of the tree reckon that Yitzhak is under a constraint on how to achieve originality as a storyteller, since he's bound to draw on much the same wellspring of experience as his elder brother. But the consensus is that, breaking new ground, he will surpass—*ibervaksen*, grow taller than—I. J. Singer. How so? He will, they say, combine realism with philosophic acceptance of the supernatural, with otherworldly elements rationalists spurn as superstition but are as inseparable from reality as is superstition from human nature. And given his gift for mockery, sarcasm, and irony, Yitzhak will provide the reader with the singular entertainment for which the literati are now waiting at the foot of the tree, at risk of being late for their own lunch.

They while the time away with sneers at I. J. Singer, the failed painter who took to writing, the Don Quixote who ran off to Kiev to liberate the oppressed proletariat and came away with his tail between his legs after the Bolshie apparatchiks threw *Perl* back in his face as unfit for print. Admittedly a gem, that novella gained him his appointment of Warsaw correspondent for the New York Yiddish daily *Forverts*, say the dacha literati, and far be it from them to begrudge his overnight leap from poverty to prosperity. But they declare themselves wise to I. J. Singer's haughty airs masking his dread fear of the flowering of Yitzhak's latent talent. He plays the role of the protective elder brother and Yitzhak that of the meek, admiring younger one, but in fact this is a sophisticated variant of the Abel and Cain theme. Yitzhak, they say, is not fooled and when it suits him will let his simmering resentment explode.

I listen to all this talk and wonder if it reaches Yitzhak's ears up there in the tree. When at last he deigns to descend he slithers down the trunk agile as a squirrel. Once on the ground he is surrounded by the literati begging for an impersonation. They offer him a choice between three celebrities—a nutty mystic, a pompous essayist, or an alcoholic poet.

Yitzhak strikes a comic scarecrow pose of bewilderment as if unable to make up his mind. Slowly the seconds—or is it minutes?—pass until we become aware that he is no longer there, that he has vanished like a phantom. Heads turn in all directions, but there is no Yitzhak; there will be no burlesque.

21. THE GRANDPARENTS

One hot early morning in that summer of 1926 I spy, escorted by Shi-ya, a black-robed skeletal wisp of a woman taking gingerly steps on the burning hot sand. She is my grandmother Bathsheva. I recognize her because my mother has so often described her to me. Age has shriveled her still-erect frame. Her neck is scrawny beyond belief and the once fiery red eyebrows are faded. The blue of the enormous sunken eyes is no bluer than the blue of the thin lips. It seems she arrived during the night with my grandfather Reb Pinhas Menahem from their distant Galician shtetl of Zykow Stary, where they had fled with young Moshe from Warsaw during the Great War.

Hastening toward her is my mother in their first encounter since they parted ways in Berlin. Bathsheva pauses out of reach of my mother's arms uplifted for an embrace. In a husky warble she declares, "Why, Hindele, you are not at all as ugly as I thought you were."

Next my grandmother, thin lips pursed, bestows a first (and last) glance at me, a boy of bar-mitzvah age, shockingly bareheaded and bare legged, shamelessly bereft of earlocks and ritual fringes.

Fascinated, I stare back at her. There is to Bathsheva more—and less—than my mother's oft-repeated portrayal of her. I am fascinated by the haggard little face, the sharp cheekbones, the prominent nose, and the upturned chin. I wonder how so small and birdlike a head can contain a brain capable of storing all those volumes of Torah, Talmud, and Kabbalah. I know because my mother has so often told me so that she cannot forgive nor abjure her Maker, who made a woman of her, she who could—who should have been—a great rabbi. To make matters worse she was cursed with a daughter, and now lost to Judaism are two of her sons. There is to those enormous eyes in that gaunt face an unearthly blend of ruthless scorn and heartbreaking self-pity that beggars the imagination.

And during this visit there is much talk of the third son, my uncle Moshe He, the youngest of the three Singer brothers, considered the *gaon*, genius of the family, a born leader, an orator. On the morrow of his bar mitzvah Moshe set about organizing a Zionist youth movement, traveling far and wide throughout Galicia preaching the return to the Promised Land. Hundreds of recruits he enlisted for aliyah duly departed—without him.

Bathsheva had set to work on him; she had decided that this son, at least, would be pious. Out of filial devotion he stayed behind. Out of frustration he went to extremes of zealotry. Day and night he sits poring over Apocrypha. At dawn, even in midwinter when the ice has to be broken, he immerses himself in the running waters of a stream to do penance for the sins he hankered after and never committed. Every Monday and Thursday he fasts and eats precious little the rest of the week. He refused to travel to Swider lest he find himself seated in a crowded railway compartment where his flesh might come in contact with female flesh.

Bathsheva is proud of her achievement; her other children deplore it.

Says Shiya through gritted teeth, "Our mother has broken Moshe's spirit, and his health is ruined."

Yitzhak adds in a tone of resignation: "Our mother congratulates herself on having saved his soul from the everlasting hellfire into which we, her other children, will be cast."

"Our mother has snuffed out the will to live in her Moishele; she has buried him alive," says my mother, indignant but not the least surprised.

Now and then I catch a glimpse of my grandfather, whose appearance is everything I expected—and more so. Frail, he has the dainty tread of a ballerina disguised in rabbinic garb, black caftan, black skullcap, ritual fringes, golden earlocks bobbing to and fro, and a wavy, golden beard glued to a sweet, girlish face.

Daily I watch Yitzhak and his mother taking a stroll in the pinewoods.

They have little to say to each other although—or maybe because—they're so much alike. Pale, thin, phantomlike, they both brood ruthless scorn in the same chill, steel-blue eyes.

When he goes strolling with his father, on the other hand, Yitzhak is transformed. He spends hours listening to Reb Pinhas Menahem, and something of his father's tenderness, wonder, awe, and delight is reflected on Yitzhak's own face. He seems to be feasting on the wonders and miracles of hasidic lore.

The sky is filled with myriad stars, a full moon is risen, and Bathsheva is nowhere in sight. The evening after a fiery sunset in which the forest stands unconsumed, my grandfather musters up the courage to approach me. He halts within touching distance and gazes in quest, I suppose, of some resemblance to the Singer family. I gaze back. Never before have I seen, nor shall ever see again, such childlike lovingness in a grown man or such a look of innocence but also wisdom as in those gentle blue eyes. His red lips stir and he says to me in a tremolo, "I dearly love your mother, and you, Moshe, her dear son, I dearly love too." And with that he turns away.

The next day I do not see my grandparents. They have left the way they came—unannounced.

22. SUMMER'S END

Autumn is in the air. A solitary crow settles on the veranda rail and caws.

Yitzhak, at Shiya's request, takes his sister and myself to a Yiddish theater in Warsaw running a farce called *Redaktor Katchke—Editor Duck*. The title is funny, *katchke* being the Yiddish equivalent of the French *canard*, meaning a whopping journalistic lie. There is one gag, endlessly repeated and unfailingly raising a laugh. Every time the apoplectic editor opens his mouth he splutters a deluge of spittle, forcing the other characters to shield themselves behind straw hats or parasols.

Uncle Shiya obtained only two complimentary tickets at the box office, so Yitzhak has modestly squeezed the three of us into two seats, though there are vacant places on either side of us. After a while I get bored and my interest strays to Yitzhak, who does not give the stage so much as a single glance. Evidently he considers this cheap fare good enough for us, while he himself gazes away into nothingness. I want to be angry with him but can't. Somehow he is out of reach, absent, even while his jagged bones poke into me. So constant is this air of his that at table it wouldn't be surprising if he poured a spoonful of soup into his ear instead of his mouth. But he never does. He's all there, even when his temples frenziedly twitch and flush and break out into a clammy sweat. Plainly, all manner of potent, contradictory forces are at war within him, liable to throw him into convulsions but evenly matched; they call a truce, and then, for all his feverish restlessness, he has poise.

After the show he takes us to Shiya's apartment on elegant Leszna Street, where we spend the night. Early the next morning, back from shopping for breakfast, my mother and I enter with a borrowed front door key. And we are greeted by an astonishing sight.

There in the hall, on the polished parquet floor, stands Yitzhak, suffering what looks to be a crucifixion of sorts. His arms are outstretched to their full length and effectively nailed in place by on one side a skinny young woman who has dug her fingernails into the wrist she is clutching and, on the other side, a plump girl who is doing the same. Each wants him solely for herself. They wage a desperate tug of war, which bids fair to split him clean down the middle, half a Yitzhak being better than no Yitzhak at all. On his gaunt, flushed face is the smile of resignation of a mock martyr. Must I feel sorry for him? I have a hunch that, of the three, it is he who will emerge unscathed.

The one glorious summer of my early life draws to a close. Yitzhak sees us off to the station in Warsaw, and once again the two kisses he darts at my mother's cheek miss their mark. She and I stand in the corridor of the train. She waves goodbye through the open window but, shortsighted, she fails to see that he has long since vanished from the platform.

Porters slam the doors shut. The steam engine blasts its whistle. With a jolt we are on the move on steel rails that, I tell myself, stretch away uninterrupted to the English Channel and on which I promise myself, sooner rather than later, to be back again.

Again I shall breathe in the honey-sweet air of the Swider pinewoods. Again on a Sabbath outing to Otwock I shall see the fat Hasidic rebbe, in his black satin caftan, white knee-length socks, and big sable shtreimel perched rakishly on his perplexed head, escorted by a company of Hasidim flaunting all colors of beards and performing the weirdest, most entertaining ballet imaginable. And while they dance as none but they can dance, I shall again see on the same Sabbath on the outskirts of the same Otwock a pack of several hundred secular shtetl youths driving a football on and on toward a goal beyond the horizon. Again I shall see Jews who do not pretend to be other than Jews, and what a picturesque varied lot they are, these Polish Jews, from the luminary to the thief, from the rich merchant to the ragged peddler. Again in Warsaw I shall see, coated thick with beggars, the regal flights of stone stairs leading up to the massive churches. But next time, so help me, I shall make sure to see what I have left unseen of the *alte heim*, teeming with life.

It's good to be alive!

23. THE HOMECOMING

Memory reenacts the Beresford Road homecoming in a lowly parody of grand opera.

Act I

The kitchen. Enter my mother and I for a lax, one-arm embrace by my father. His other arm points at Pussy, who, dutifully fed, delivered a litter of kittens in our absence.

I place a saucer of milk on the floor for the scrabble of newcomers to the Kreitman family. My mother serves supper. After eating his fill in silence, my father rises, backs away from the table, stretches himself, and bursts into song as he has never done before.

In a powerful voice he renders the melody of what I shall eventually learn is an aria of the toreador in *Carmen*. Loud and clear is his one repetitious lament: "She loves me not! She loves me not! Tra-la-la, tra-la-la!" To it he lends a lilt of mock-agonized sorrow proclaiming in effect: "Hindele loves me not! Hindele loves me not! And loving me not she ran off to her family in the *alte heim*. But her family loves her not, her family loves her not. So what else can she do but run back to me, unloved and unloving? More's the pity!"

My mother counters in mock sorrow: "I cannot believe my ears! Reb Gedalya's wastrel son could have been a cantor with a voice to shake the walls of a synagogue and to melt the hearts of the congregation if only his own heart were not bursting with hatred for the sheer love of hatred. More's the pity!"

My father returns to the table, unfolds a newspaper, and in audible mutterings studies horse-racing forms. Having selected outsiders on which to lay bets at the bookies, he then names the opera he will at-

tend at a Covent Garden matinee. He thus intimates how he enter-
tains himself when left to himself and serves notice of his intent to
go on doing exactly as he pleases. From now on, more than ever, my
father Avrum and his unloving, unloved wife Hindele will be going
their separate ways under the same roof.

Act II

On the morrow, in the entrance hall. A singsong encounter between
our landlady and my mother.

The landlady: "Hello, hello, Mrs. Kreitman, how very good to see you
back! If only you'd come sooner you could have spared me no end of
unnecessary trouble."

My mother: "What kind of trouble, Mrs. Rosenzweig? Nothing seri-
ous, I hope."

The landlady: "Those kittens! Day in, day out I've been kept busy clearing up their droppings and their piddles all over the stairs and the
landings. More than once I begged Mr. Kreitman not to let them run
loose. But how goes the Yiddish saying? 'Speak to Elohim, speak to the
wall!' It was of no use. I really missed you. So did a certain lady who
came asking for you again and again. No, she didn't leave her name.
What does she look like? A pale bundle of skin and bones with the
smirk and lisp of a retarded child."

My mother, sotto voce: "That will be Mrs. Avigail; she's married to a
eunuch."

The landlady, in an impassioned half whisper: "Many an evening it
pleased Mr. Kreitman to keep that lady company. Really, I shouldn't be
telling you this. Please forget it!"

My mother: "Don't worry, it's already forgotten! But I'm sorry to see you in such distress, Mrs. Rosenzweig. Since there's no accounting for a gentleman's taste, you shouldn't be so jealous!"

The landlady, outraged: "I, jealous?"

My mother: "No offense, no offense; I mean you're being needlessly jealous on my behalf. As for the kittens, trust me to keep them indoors."

The landlady: "Get rid of them! I'll not have them stinking up the house!"

Mrs. Rosenzweig's piqued face and the cleft of her well-fleshed bosom in a low-cut gown are flushed scarlet as she turns away. Her squat figure radiates the furious body heat of a childless woman without a bedmate—her white-haired husband, owner of a fleet of taxis, is an insomniac who spends his nights driving a taxi.

As our landlady climbs the stairs her shoes stomp a dirge aimed at the gentleman of poor taste, her ground-floor tenant: "He loved me not! He loved me not! . . ."

Act III

Outdoors. Cats' music fades into silence. The gathering darkness echoes to the ever-more-desperate refrain: "Pussy, Pussy, where are you?"

Ever since Act II, Pussy and her kittens have thrice daily been let out into the back garden and lured home with platters placed in the kitchen doorway left ajar.

But one day they fail to return, and I go in search of them in the driving rain . . .

Daybreak. As always before leaving for school I carry the overnight bag of garbage to the dustbin. There in the passageway between the back and front gardens I sight the ruffled white carcass of Pussy. Eyelids tight-shut, she lies on her side, paws outstretched as if in a last effort to leap up and run for her life. I kick away a chunk of meat, which I guess is the poisoned bait left there by the landlady.

The rationalist in me is prejudiced against funeral rites held by the living for their own consolation. It will make no difference to Pussy if I drop her remains into the dustbin. I do nothing of the kind. I pick her up, not by the scruff of the neck but tenderly cradled in both hands, carry her to a corner of the back garden, dig a muddy hole of sorts with a scrap of wood, and cover her grave with dead leaves.

I skip school and go looking for the kittens. I find none, dead or alive. At home I say nothing for fear of a breakdown of my mother into hysterics.

A scene follows in which a scraggy little white cat—no longer a kitten, but the pattern of the black tip to its tail plainly marks it as Pussy's offspring—appears on the kitchen windowsill. *Tap tap tap* goes its upraised paw on the pane. I hasten to feed it in the back garden. To allow it indoors is to risk a second poisoning. If delivered to the Society for the Prevention of Cruelty to Animals, it will be mercifully put to sleep the same as the hundreds and thousands of other strays.

What am I to do? I carry, cradled in my arms, not the stone-cold, inert Pussy but her now-warm, struggling other self all the way to upper-class Highbury. There I drop her—I cannot think of Pussy II as a tomcat—over a well-trimmed hedge into the front garden of a fine house.

The stage is set with a visionary scene of merry children who coax their mother into adopting Pussy in a household reverberating with love, more love, and still more love . . .

The memory of this episode surfaces every once in a while in the most unexpected moments for no apparent reason other than to put me to shame.

The curtains are taken down in our parlor. A notice is pasted on the window: TO LET.

24. LORDSHIP PARK

"You know foon a goot plumber, en'it?"

Shosha, our new landlady, thus addresses herself to the postman come to deliver letters at the front door.

"Missus," says the goy, who doesn't know a Hasidic chant when he hears one, "who ever heard of a good plumber?"

The duet, performed on the stage of the Pavillion Theatre in White-chapel, could have an audience in stitches. For my part, I am more than amused. Shosha—as landladies go I couldn't wish for a better one—strikes an ancestral chord in me. Her trust in imminent deliverance from a leaky water pipe matches my no less innocent belief in the forthcoming brotherhood of man. Torrents of blood will flow under the bridges, mountains of human ashes be scattered to the winds, state-of-the-art genocide and suicidal folly will prevail ere I, a slow learner, grasp the Torah concept of Cain and Abel brotherliness. In later life at odd moments àpropos of nothing and everything I shall often hear myself wistfully echoing Shosha's incantation: "You know foon a goot plumber, en'it?"

Our present address is Lordship Park, a ground-floor flat in a house no different from Beresford Road except that Beresford will always remind me of burial, my burial of Pussy. Names have charms. Any doubts in the matter will finally be dispelled for me in Jerusalem by rabbis who, well versed in Cabala, unfailingly prescribe a change of name for all chronic ailments and woes. Were I called Shimon, which happily I'm not, I'd be well advised straightway to assume some other name, since Satan has his evil eye fixed on each and every Shimon. Why? The devil alone knows.

Though we live in Lordship Park, a stone's throw away from Queen Elizabeth Walk, far be it from me to entertain queenly or lordly expectations. Life takes its inevitable course for better and for worse.

My mother, the first of the Singer siblings to have taken up the pen, writes short stories about the *alte heim* peopled with characters I never heard of in the tales she told me—Jewish peasants and artisans and shlemiels, good-for-nothings. Deeming herself the outcast of the Singer family, she signs her stories "Esther Kreitman," and I read them in pre-Sabbath issues of one or another of the two Yiddish dailies, the *Tzeit* or the *Post*.

Friday mornings, with a dab of lipstick to her lips, she goes to collect her honorarium—she so terms the several welcome shillings she's paid—and joins the weekly assembly of journalists and literati in a Whitechapel café. When I come home from school she has harsh words for these scribblers who respect her writings but not the writer.

On Saturday nights she takes me along to the Yiddish-speaking Workers' Circle in the East End. There I play chess and listen to the bickerings, in which my mother feverishly takes part, between Socialists and Communists. She comes away vexed.

My mother is befriended by the same Mrs. Avigail, married to a eunoch, the landlady in Beresford Road complained about. She is a tall wisp of a woman whose breasts—I wonder if she has any—give no sign of themselves in her starched white blouse. From its lacy collar rises a slender stalk upholding a wan flower in the semblance of a girlish face framed with gossamer blonde hair. Elfish feet in pink shoes peep forth from the hem of her black skirt like parched tongues. I have yet to see in the National Gallery a medieval painting of so wraithlike a Virgin Mary.

Mrs. Avigail is indeed a virgin, or so she murmurs—in my hearing—at my mother. She pitter-patters on and on how dearly she loves and is loved by her husband who, alas, is impotent. I look Mr. Avigail over. A towering bundle of gnarled bones wearing a fierce, dark moustache, he is to my guileless mind the very image of a rapist.

On alternate Sundays my mother and I take tea with the Avigails in their immaculate drawing room, and she, without her beloved husband, comes to tea in our shabby, genteel parlor. When my father is present she darts timid glances in his direction but, bedazzled, never looks straight at him. In his absence she shyly eyes me from head to foot. My groin stirs.

I down a cup of tea, stuff Petit Beurre and digestive biscuits into my mouth, politely excuse myself, and go off to the river Lea. A strenuous hour on a rowboat relieves me of my erotic fantasies. I then take a riverside stroll far into the night past gigantic gasometers, piles of garbage, waste ground fringed by rough slums, and, with clenched fists, stride through clusters of sinister loungers.

In my dreams at night the puny Lea broadens into a mysterious river, and I cross a pillared bridge into an outlandish town, the likes of which I have never ever seen or imagined in my waking hours.

The weeks, the months, the seasons pass. Now my mother's epileptic fits are few and far between. Another year goes by and she suffers none. In their stead it's as if the seizures have spread themselves into senseless furies and anguished broodings.

I grow up choosing to ignore the fact that I owe my existence to the dybbuk or sick alter ego implanted in my mother at birth by her own mother Bathsheva, who mercilessly cast away an unwanted daughter, a Hindele who eventually resigned herself to a mismatch with Avrum. And I, their offspring, feel it my duty to look after her and even feel sorry for him who smiles at me but who has never cared for me.

At school I hold my own. I matriculate. The headmaster sets the class a competitive essay on John Bunyan's *The Pilgrim's Progress*. I marvel at the utter madness, sublimating a widespread mental disorder, that drove the Pilgrim through "Sloughs of Despond" toward the kingdom of Christ where dwell "the Elders with their golden Crowns, the Holy Virgins with their golden Harps, men that by the World were cut in pieces, burnt in flames, eaten of beasts, drowned in the Seas, for the Love that they bare to the Lord of the place; all well, and cloathed with Immortality as with a garment." I also marvel at Bunyan's spells of lucidity offering peerless down-to-earth portrayals of the mortals he encounters on his pilgrimage.

I expect bad marks due the unbelieving Jew that I am. Instead I receive the prize copy of the book, bearing the inscription: "Awarded to Mr. Kreitman for Essay on John Bunyan, Dr. W. G. Sleight, Headmaster, Stoke Newington Central School, Jan. 1929."

Dr. Sleight bestows on me a testimonial stating, among other accomplishments, that I played football for my school, never mind that I did so in only one game at center forward without scoring or even taking a potshot at the goal. With this charitable tribute to my sportsmanship I go out into the world with high hopes of finding a job as junior clerk in a reputable city firm.

I scan the Situations Vacant columns in the morning papers, make written applications, and while the time away reading the daily news. Duly impressed with the installation of a first-ever Labour government after the general strike and with the promise of social justice at long last, nothing so touches me to the quick as the report of a common-place crime. A schoolmaster is convicted of sexually molesting his girl pupils and is let off with a suspended one-year prison sentence. I know that schoolmaster. He is my old acquaintance, my tormentor, Mr. Baker.

I am summoned for interviews. I appear in my dry-cleaned Fifty Shil-lings Tailors navy blue serge suit, a striped Marks and Spencer's tie, polished black True-Form shoes newly soled and heeled. I have been to the barber's for a sixpenny haircut, and my manner is bright, my conduct modest.

Soon I need another haircut. I've already had two. I decide not to both-er with a third. I take a tram to London Docks. I turn into a long street lined on one side by a long wall sky-high under the lowering sky. I hear the sirens of ships on the Thames. I see an Italian name, Napolitano Bros., Ltd., painted above the boarded-up ground-floor windows of a grimy corner house.

The entrance is up a steep alley. An outlandish odor, spicy and musty, pervades the inner gloom. I raise the flap of a barrier, lower it behind me, and pause. Ahead is a staircase. There are also two doors. One leads down to a wine cellar. The other opens into a warehouse stocked with barrels on the floor, jars and tins on the shelves, fat sausages and huge cheeses hooked to the ceiling.

"Who you lookin' for, mate? The what, the managin' director? The boss, 'e sits on his arse one floor up," says an obliging warehouseman.

Upstairs I am told to wait at the open door of the managing director's office. He sits leaning over papers on his desk. Every once in a while he gets up and, in the same leaning posture but loudly snapping his fingers, strides on tiptoe into the general office. He wears dark overalls and a gold watch chain on his natty black waistcoat. On his return, no longer snapping his fingers, he brushes up against me and the doorpost. He doesn't look my way, but a contact is established. I feel he doesn't like me any more than I like him.

I wait and wait. There is to his person an outlandish aura, a sizzling heat that engraves his appearance into my mind and to no purpose, I suppose, since I'm only waiting to be sent packing. But I shan't forget those flamelike black curls on his head, the bushy black eyebrows, the crafty bloodshot eyes, the upturned sniffy nostrils, the fleshy bluish lips, and with it all, that rare swarthy complexion, a cross between a black olive and a green olive aglow with a flush of disdain.

At last an upraised forefinger beckons me in. I stand before him. He shuffles through his papers without looking up at me, demands in rhythmic Italianized English particulars of my family life, plays deaf to my startled answers, frowns at my claim to prowess in shorthand typing, says "Thirty shillings a week," rises, and in his accustomed leaning posture strides past me, this time snapping his fingers at me behind his back.

I follow him into the general office, where he points at a desk with a type-writer on it next to the time-recording clock. In a tone of sweet mockery he inquires, "Are you a slacker, Jerry, or what is it?" and turns away.

In a waking dream I descend the creaking stairs, pass the barrier, open the door, step into the chill rain sweeping litter down the steep alley, and, soaked to the skin before I reach the tram terminus, collect my wits.

Emptyhanded I went out into the world. And I'm in it at thirty bob a week!

25. THE FIRST JOB

Dreamland doesn't hold a candle to dockland. The outlandish river-side town of my past dreams pales beside the shabby corner house where I go to work. As well compare the fantasy feast of a beggar with a real meal that nourishes even while it sickens body and soul.

Where would I, Jerry the slacker, and my fellow Jerry the slackers be without it? "Out in the gutter," says finger-snapping Togni _____.

We weren't born yesterday and need no such reminder. Irrespective of age from under fourteen to over seventy, we slack away for all we are worth and look up to our provider and forward to Friday payday, overtime unpaid. Togni's two brothers are also kept on wages but are honored with names of their own. The elder brother, mild and meek Giovanni, is the keeper of the wine cellar. The eldest, big brash Carlo, serves as salesman and collector of bad debts.

I slack away on the letters that Togni dictates at a dizzying speed and I dutifully anglicize on the typewriter. His clientele of specialized restaurants and brothels are Italians, Greeks, Spaniards, and several Frenchwomen, who occasionally drop in to vent their outrage at the high prices he charges for delicatessen obtainable nowhere else. On such occasions Togni responds in English that seems impeccable compared to their own abuse of the language.

When he is busy in the warehouse or down in the cellar or up on the top floor, where old files are locked away and where the walls are hung with portraits of bemedaled field marshals who waged forgotten wars, we slackers in the general office take time off from credits and debits for laughter and sighs. The accountant wonders what awaits us all in our next resurrection and is crushed by the cry in chorus: "Bookkeeper!" The septuagenarian warming his bald pate at the gas fire at the risk of singeing the ends of his gray moustache waxes nostalgic over better days. The old boozer, whose business it is to press home trumped-up insurance claims, blends Shakespearean rhetoric with lewd expletives in shafts of mockery aimed at one and all, but more especially at the veteran head clerk, who turns a deaf ear—the one that had its drum blasted in the trenches of Flanders. The "bloody Dago" Togni is thoroughly vilified and grudgingly admired for both his shrewdness and his clowning. The mirth and the moans are as repetitious as Togni's inquiry on his return: "Are you slacking, Jerry, or what is it?"

I listen and get to hear of Togni's life story and the history of the corner house. The old-timers have the lowdown from Carlo, whose jealousy of his young brother overrides discretion. The family boast of aristocratic descent and ruin brought on by a dissolute count is debatable. That the parents arrived from Naples poor as church mice and are now running a cheap lodging house in Cardiff is unquestionable.

Togni, still in his teens, married a crippled girl for her dowry, spent it on fake Renaissance paintings and portraits of famed warriors with which he decamped to Paris, ran into trouble, and came to London. Here he set himself up as an importer of Italian marble for tombstones in a shed rented from and adjoining the corner house. The landlord, a Greek whose wholesale trade in foodstuffs was a cover for espionage, fled the country on the outbreak of the Great War. Togni then knocked a hole into a brick wall, fitted a door, took over the premises, established Napolitano Bros., Ltd., and flourished.

The errand boy Jerry—all the errand boys engaged by Togni are called Jerry, as we are—has this to tell of the boss's suburban villa to which he makes deliveries. Mrs. Napolitano, an Englishwoman and a peach with a lovely little son, is allowed a daily charwoman but not a live-in maid. The garden is tended and odd jobs about the house are done by an earlier Jerry, now a grown man who, poor chap, has to wear a collapsible top hat that Togni flattens whenever the fancy takes him.

All days in the corner house are much of a muchness. A few minutes past six I'm the first to clock out. When I pass Togni's ever-open door he may or may not jump up at me from his revolving chair. But he knows a stubborn ass when he sees one. So I go on my way past the barrier, down the creaky stairs, past another barrier, out of the door, down the alley, and turn right into the main street. There on wet days I hug the walls to not get splashed with mud by passing lorries and horse-drawn carts. On Fridays I step aside from the young and not-so-young women who stand propped up against walls and lampposts with scarlet cheeks and unbuttoned coats and silk stockings drawn negligently over shapeless or swollen legs as though tired of forever dressing and undressing.

They croon: "Not tonight, darling? All right, duckie!"

I give a wide berth to the middle-aged woman posted outside the red-brick mission house with its washed-out poster at either end: THE VITAL QUESTION: ARE YOU SAVED? She doesn't need rouge on one cheek eaten away by bluish scarlet rot. I promise myself never, ever to use the services of a prostitute. I have already masturbated in bed, half awake and half asleep, but sooner that than syphilis.

In the winter I leave home in the dark and return in the dark. One evening I find my mother packing a suitcase. "I am going to Warsaw," she says, offering no explanation, and I ask for none. My attempts at dissuasion are halfhearted.

After she has had the Belgian and German visas stamped in her Polish passport I suggest she put off her departure to Sunday so I shan't have to take time off from the office. My father's offer to accompany her to Victoria Station is snubbed. On the bus ride my mother broods, and I can't think of anything to say.

I carry her suitcase into the waiting train, stoop for a hasty parting kiss, and from the platform I wave at the carriage window from which she smiles back at me. My mother is gone, but her smile lingers and hurts. A blind woman dispensing herself of the services of a guide dog straining at the leash might indulge in just such a smile. Sooner than later, I suppose, she will be back. Meanwhile I'm off the leash.

My father and I agree to share the housework. When business is slack he'll do the shopping and what little cooking and cleaning there is. In the busy season—and Christmas is coming soon—I'll take over.

I'm up and about with the next-door cockerel, who can't wait for daylight, or else he reckons he's a night bird. I listen to the wireless, to the chimes of Big Ben followed by anxious news bulletins telling of poverty, unemployment, a world in confusion and disarray. I also tune in to the crackle of foreign stations.

I get to dockland before the eight o'clock siren scatters the pigeons from the ledge of my corner house and from wherever else they are roosting. The tiny gates in the opposite sky-high wall open. Hundreds of dockers hustle in, and minutes later, countless hundreds shuffle out—"out into the gutter," as Togni would say. A few ships wait to be loaded or unloaded.

I find my way to the long flight of stone stairs down to the Thames and, if it's not raining, sit watching the dark-gray sheet of water, ruffled, as if flowing over a cobbled highway lined on the farther side by huge warehouses, chimneyed factories, and in their midst a church with a cross on its slender spire. Tiny seagulls are afloat, and when one for no reason at all—or waking from a nightmare?—flies upward, turning into a large, screeching angry bird, all the others follow.

Evenings, when the woman whose bluish-scarlet left cheek has me scared isn't in the doorway of the mission house, I stand there listening to the click of billiard balls and the excited jabber of foreign seamen at play. If I weren't underage I might drop in at the uproarious pub where the writer of Togni's fraudulent insurance claims stands at the counter guzzling his beer in grim silence.

At home I sit up late reading. Often I borrow from the Church Street public library my best-loved novels, short stories, plays. Turgenev, who used to be my favorite, still charms but doesn't move me the way Chekhov does. Saturday nights I go to the cinema; I can't afford theaters. And Sundays I roam around London in all weather. Dockland isn't the only outlandish district in the gray metropolis.

My mother's letters wax rapturous. She spends entire days in the Yiddish Writers' Club on Tlomackie Street, and there she is at home as nowhere else ever before. The editor of the daily *Express* has accepted her stories of the *alte heim* and has asked for sketches of Jewish life in London. She has found a true friend in Runya, Yitzhak's sweetheart, not that he deserves her, who is so warmhearted, and he so heartless. Perhaps I remember the plump girl in Shiya's flat the morning after Yitzhak took us to see that silly play *Redaktor Katchke?* She is Runya. I do remember her, and I also remember the skinny girl and their tug-of-war on Yitzhak's outstretched arms.

I try my hand at a short story. A tramp I saw last summer crouched up against a tree by the river Lea and reading a book through cracked spectacles scurries for shelter from the autumn rain into a cellar, where he lies bundled up in rags and rats leap on and over him for the crumbs of a stale chunk of bread he was nibbling.

I haven't heard of Knut Hamsun's masterly novel *Hunger*, and that's the title I give to my story, which enchants me in the writing and disenchants me when I reread it. Acceptable is the riverside part of straightforward description shot through with imagination, with the thoughts and the feelings and the memories of the studious tramp.

Unacceptable is the follow-up in the cellar, mere make-believe. Where draw the line between imagination and make-believe? It's arbitrary.

26. END OF MY FIRST JOB

The routine hilarity in the general office when Togni is not around is interrupted by a warehouseman.

"Alf," he says, "'as gone and done it!"

"Done what, Charlie?"

"Given the boss a smack on the kisser!"

"You don't say!"

"You 'eard me!"

I follow Charlie as far as the landing. Below all is quiet. Back in the hushed office I look out of a window into the alley for the arrival of a doctor, an ambulance, the police. Nothing.

I see—the next best thing to hearing—the song of the caged canary in an opposite wide-open window. Once again I wonder if Burglar Bill, so named by the neighbors but really only a petty thief, retrieved his old pet bird when he got out of prison or bought, if he couldn't steal, a new one. Its bright yellow plumes shame the brassy tint of the sun hanging above the rooftops like one of the three balls—two are missing—of a pawnbroker's sign.

The "smack on the kisser," when we get to hear more about it, is by common consent a letdown. Alf, the driver of the delivery van, did raise his fist but unclenched it to land nothing worse than a flip, a caress of sorts on Togni's cheek. He lost his temper after Togni teased him, not for the first time, about his bandaged eye, saying it would go blind with filth picked up from whores.

"Alf jist then," Charlie explains, "was angry with the 'orspital doctors tellin' 'im to piss off an' go fetch the undertaker for 'is kid. An' now 'e's out on 'is neck wi' three more kids to feed."

At the downstairs barrier, a few days later, the woman wearing a strip of black crepe is Alf's wife, begging: "Please, sir, may 'e come in an' see the boss an' tell 'im 'ow terribly sorry 'e is?"

"Madam, how many more times must I tell you that Mr. Napolitano is out?" says Mr. Blade, the septuagenarian of the drooping gray moustache.

She picks up the infant clinging to her skirts and seats her, a frilly little girl, on the flap of the barrier.

Togni stands on an upper landing—and I lurk behind him—looking on.

A plea of "Alf's 'urt pride" raises a chortle from Mr. Blade and a long, drawn-out wail from the child. The mother strokes her cheek.

I slink away, look out of the window, see Alf loitering in the alley. I go back to my desk and from that day on become the spoilsport of revelry in the general office. I spout inanities about human dignity and social equity that trigger great hilarity, and the ensuing chorus of "Up with everything that's down! And down with everything that's up!" cannot quell me.

Mr. Blade, the appeaser, says, "Our young'un next to the recording clock has a point—live and let live! That's the secret of making big money. Togni doesn't understand that. I don't suppose he ever will."

"Swindle and let swindle, you mean!" I correct him. "And don't forget to laugh your head off at 'urt pride."

Mr. Blade, the appeaser, is also the informer. Charlie knows it and never opens up in his presence. Come Friday, I'm not overly surprised when Togni inquires with mock gravity as he strides past me, snapping his fingers: "Are you an anarchist, Jerry, or what is it?"

With bowed head Mr. Miller, the head clerk of the deaf ear, bids me the first time ever to sign a receipt for my last-ever pay. I'm out on my neck without a week's notice and, worse, without references from Napolitano Bros., Ltd.

27. THE NEW JOB

An absurd fancy takes me to answer an advertisement seeking a free-lance translator of German patent specifications into English. Having no qualifications, I state none in my written application. Nevertheless summoned to the office of the British Thomson Houston Company in Bush House on Southampton Row, I am entrusted with the trial trans-lation of several patents of the Allgemeine Elektricitäts Gesellschaft. The BTH and the AEG are respectively the foremost producers of so-phisticated electrical instruments in Britain and Germany.

I stop off at Foyles' bookshop to invest in a heavy German-English dictionary. In it I look up words that are new to me. For the rest I rely on my homely Yiddish to deduce the meaning of German intricacies. I submit what to me is mumbo jumbo and thereafter receive as much work as I can cope with. The pay is handsome, at a fixed rate for a given number of lines.

In the coming years I'll no longer buy my navy blue serge suits at the Fifty Shilling Tailors. Savile Row at a pinch may be within my means, but there's a limit to absurdity, which I daren't overstep.

My mother returns, dispirited, to Lordship Park. Though she did not write to say she was coming, I have been expecting her. For the first half year of her stay in Warsaw her letters, accompanied by clippings of her published stories, were aglow with the bliss of the companionship she basked in far into the night among the literati frequenting the Yiddish Writers' Club on Tlomackie Street. There she belonged and nowhere else. Tacitly she had bade a firm adieu to her unloved husband and to me, her beloved son.

Then came more letters, still with clippings attached, but the tone toward me had changed, had become doting, affectionate, too affectionate, which sounded an alarm bell within me. It seemed redolent of a relapse into loneliness and its miseries.

Now that my mother has me all day at home at work on my Underwood typewriter, again and again she begins to tell me what went wrong in and out of Tlomackie Street. First comes Runya, whose distress she shares. Runya has been left in the lurch after bearing Yitzhak a son. She is a Communist and was thinking of taking her fatherless little boy to the Soviet Union. But on second thought she preferred a kibbutz in Zion, where a revolution was wanted—a revolution waged by the Jews shoulder to shoulder with their Arab cousins against Zionism and against the mandatory regime of imperialist Britain.

I am not content with this explanation. I wait and wait for more than dribs and drabs of an answer to my unasked question: What happened beyond the point at which she repeatedly stops short in her fulminations at the duplicity of her Tlomackie Street cronies, more especially the double-dealing, the treachery, of a go-getter writer, an obsequious, deceitful, insincere scribbler who went down on his knees to her as a writer and made a fool of her behind her back?

Since my mother does not wish me to know precisely what passed between him and her, I, her son, do not wish to know. So I tell myself. But the brain is characterized in that it is composed of many more zones than the conscious, the subconscious, and the unconscious. There are bound to be multiple compartments to process separately the multitude of mixed feelings, and only then does the brain, if possible, reconcile the resultant conflicting notions. Without these zones the human being is subject to all manner of afflictions, from imbecile passivity to raging hysteria and downright madness. I do not for a moment suppose that this is my patented discovery. Not having read Freud, Jung, and Adler—but I have read *about* them—I flatter myself that, uninfluenced by my betters, I can think things out for myself.

There is, of course, one zone or compartment given to workings of the imagination, either creative or morbid or both, giving rise at best to great works of art and at worst to pestilential myths. Much as I, an aspiring storyteller, cherish my imagination, I am also wary of it. Right now if I let it run loose, it will work up a nasty carnal liaison between my mother Hindele and that go-getter scribbler whom she calls an *oysvurf*, a cad. The seeds of such a fantasy are sown, no two ways about it, and sprout they will sooner or later—hopefully later, much later.

My mother, for her part, addresses her imagination to the writing of a quasi-autobiographical novel, and she entitled it *Der Shaidim Tantz— The Dance of the Demons.*

I take time off from AEG patent specifications to put together a long short story, "Winter Death." It opens with "Mr. Hirsh was an old man when he died." He is drawn from life, but I never saw him die. I have a hangup on death. Maybe dead cats have something to do with it.

In principle, all work and no play should make me, no longer a shabby teenager but a smart young man of twenty, a first-class bore. And in practice that is what I am, no two ways about it.

My mother, whose epileptic fits are now few and far between but whose dybbuk aggravates her neurosis, clings to the apron string of her only child. Not that I, her son, do the housework. Thanks to my salary we now have a cleaning lady, and my mother takes care of the cooking. The shopping is my chore. Mornings, after a night of mostly erotic dreams, I make my bed, the front parlor couch, on which I masturbate. I have a crush on womanhood, but not on any particular woman. When I go to the cinema in the evening I'm not even in love with Greta Garbo.

On occasion I entertain myself with vague thoughts of suicide. In real earnest, however, the fun without which my life wouldn't be worth living I derive from work, at which I'm a maniac, no less.

Apart from my translations I have lovingly begun to draft a novel. I shall call it *The House of Napolitano*, modeled on my adventures in the Napolitano Brothers firm.

My mother receives an inscribed copy of her brother Shiya's first novel, *Shtool oon Eizen* (*Steel and Iron*, a Yiddish figure of speech for *ruthlessness*), a description of war and revolution in Eastern Europe. The Warsaw critics, who loathe him, have panned it ruthlessly. And he has reacted with a letter to the editor of the local daily, *Das Heint*, announcing in a single sentence his "renunciation of Yiddish literature."

I. J. Singer will renounce his renunciation with, among other works, his superb family saga *The Brothers Ashkenazi* and his masterly comic novel *Yoshe Kalb*, which he will dramatize. Maurice Schwartz will direct and act in it, and it will be the longest-ever-running play, staged several years in New York prior to a worldwide tour.

Thinking it over, my heart warms to my uncle's outrageous fit of pique, to the likes of which I am prone but only to suppress them. I set about translating *Steel and Iron*, change the title to *Blood Harvest*, submit the typescript to a literary agent, and, published by Sampson Low, it garners a harvest of favorable reviews.

Then I dream up an anthology of Jewish short stories. The idea appeals to Faber & Faber, who will eventually publish it entitled *Jewish Short Stories of Today*. Of the twenty-eight stories I select, eight are in Yiddish, which I translate. Two are by my uncles. From promising young Yitzhak's first novel, *The Satan in Goray*, I excerpt a self-contained passage, calling it "Hail, the Messiah!" And he makes his first appearance in English under a pseudonym, Yitzhak Bashevis—minus Singer. I include a story by Esther Kreitman, "The Relic," plus my own "Winter Death" under a nom de plume, Martin Lea. Thus four different names serve to disguise a flagrant family affair. As editor I sign Morris Kreitman.

In my ten-page introduction I excuse the omission of American authors on the grounds that they are already well known. I deemed it best to fill this space with work that has never reached the English reader before. Among the Russian, German, and French celebrities are Boris Pasternak, Ilya Ehrenburg, Franz Kafka, Stefan Zweig, Lion Feuchtwanger, Ernst Toller, André Maurois, Henri Duvernois (whom I translate from the French), and, questionably, Marcel Proust.

I fail to explain my choice of Proust, a churchgoing Catholic. I am certainly not motivated by halakha, the rabbinic law, which qualifies as a Jew anyone who has a Jewish mother. Proust's mother is also a practicing Catholic. What's more, Proust utterly ignores his Jewish origins in "A la recherche du temps perdu," literally "in search of time lost" but usually translated as "in remembrance of things past." Arguably, stretching a far-fetched point, the Proustian style of hair-splitting analysis, exhaustive and even exhausting, is akin to Talmudic pilpul. My excuse for picking on Proust's "Sole Mio" is reverence for his storytelling genius, his enrichment of creative literature in the portrayal of a snob, a social parasite.

I too am in dread of time lost. While writing my own novel I set about translating my mother's.

The English P.E.N. Club sets up a Young P.E.N. Club. I enter a competition for new members and am awarded first prize for "Winter Death." My mother keeps me company at the meetings of young new writers, and I drop out.

I go on keeping her company for her evening visits to the Yiddish Workers' Circle in the East End. There she is received with due respect for Esther Kreitman, whose stories they enjoy in the pre-Sabbath newspapers. I play chess while waiting for her.

She does not wish me to attend when every Friday noon she goes to a Whitechapel café where Yiddish writers gather in the august presence of Morris Meyer, editor of *Die Tzeit*.

I then go rowing on the river Lea.

28. THE TRIP TO PARIS

My mother wishes me to go to Paris, alone without her, and there distribute copies of her novel *Der Shaidim Tantz*. At the end of last winter she submitted her manuscript to the éminence grise of Yiddish publishers in Warsaw, Ch. Brzoza, and now in the summer of '36 the book is out, a paperback in beautiful print and not a word of the original text changed.

She speaks of my forthcoming solo trip with an air of finality, and I do hope she won't at the last moment change her mind. It is the better part of wisdom not to look a gift horse in the mouth. Yet I cannot help wondering what can have induced her to let me off the leash. I guess her considerations are—like my metaphors—mixed. After her misadventures in Warsaw, she is apparently resigned to staying put in Lordship Park, a few houses off Queen Elizabeth Walk. At the same time, her attitude to me has taken an ambivalent turn. Inscribed on the flyleaf of her presentation copy of *Dance of the Demons,* bound in green leather, I read to my dismay: "To my dear son and eminent colleague Moshe Kreitman from Esther Kreitman." With a touch of condescension my mother has upgraded me into two sons in one. Last and by no means least, if at twenty-three I am still a virgin, then must she not bear part of the blame?

Her presence at Young P.E.N. Club meetings, which I no longer attend, served to nip in the bud, or so she fancies, a romance with a budding poetess. This bespectacled and overweight young lady flaunting a silver cross on her generous decolleté made passes at me. A golden Star of David wouldn't have appealed to my mother either. An attachment that would detach me from her lonely self is the very last thing she wants.

If I read my mother's mind right, she is sending me off to Paris, the city of lights and easy love, in the hope that without her at my side I will at last have my fling "doin' what comes natural," as prescribed in a jazz number dear to the BBC. Hope springs eternal. Hers, I believe, is assorted with doubts of my virility. I could, but of course I don't, reassure her by telling of my "journeys" at the age of eight on top of nine-year-old Helen. Although I have already promised myself to break loose from my possessive mother, I had wanted to do so of my own accord, not hers. For the present, I say nothing and am content to bide my time.

Meanwhile, I have a gallivanting father who often brings home a whiff of cheap scent from a declared night out at the greyhound races. On all such occasions my mother merely remarks, "Avrum is gone to the dogs."

With a kiss on the forehead from her and a wave of the hand from him I set off on my travels. And, as the Yiddish idiom has it, "like last year's snow" out of sight and out of mind are morbid thoughts of sex when, alone amid hundreds of fellow passengers, I take the train to Dover, board the ferry boat to Calais, catch the express to Paris, alight at the Gare du Nord, at a news kiosk pick up *Le Figaro*, the two Yiddish dailies *Die Neie Presse* and *Unzer Vort*, and, elated, step out into the great city.

It is late afternoon, and bursts of sunshine break through lowering clouds, setting the city aglow with beckoning mysteries. I survey a row of sooty seven-story buildings. Behind each shut or shuttered window lurk characters awaiting the pen of a latter-day Balzac. And in some houses with a double tier of garrets are iron bedsteads not only for *femmes de chambre* but also for avant-garde artists whose paintings will hang in museums after they're dead.

I look at the street signs. I'm in Rue La Fayette, and the traffic is resonant with the demolition of the Bastille and the Franco-American War of Independence. I come to a busy thoroughfare with single-decker buses greener than the leaves of the plane trees lining either pavement of Boulevard de Magenta, which intrigues me all the more in that I know not who or what Magenta is.

I book in at a modest hotel and deposit my suitcase in a small, sparsely furnished room. I hear a peal of thunder and, with it, the call of duty.

I put on my raincoat, pick up my briefcase normally reserved for patent specifications, go downstairs, and in my heavily accented French, ask my way to Paradis.

The receptionist looks at me. I can see him saying to himself, "Another nutty Englishman." I elaborate, "Rue du Paradis." He corrects me: "Rue *de* Paradis." Then he tells me that if after Magenta, opposite the church, I turn into rue de la Fidélité, that will take me "tout droit au Paradis," straight into paradise. He is obviously delighted with his own witty remark.

The old church stands where it has stood for centuries, graced by a stony Jesus flanked by his Apostles. Rue de Paradis is a narrow, quaintly shoddy street. Number 14 displays a plaque in Yiddish, *Die Neie Presse*, and in French, *La Presse Nouvelle*. It is my first choice, a Communist daily with a larger circulation than the Zionist *Unser Wort*.

I enter and introduce myself: the son of Esther Kreitman, the sister of I. J. Singer. The editor welcomes me and shows off the flesh-and-blood nephew to assistants who are in and out of his office with copy for his scrutiny. The phone keeps ringing. I down the cup of coffee I've been offered, hand over a copy of *Der Shaidim Tantz*, and am seen off to the door with a handshake and a piece of advice: the time and place to meet the Yiddish literati is midmorning in the Café Thénint on Place de la République.

I leave *Unser Wort* for tomorrow. I walk the length of Rue de Paradis, where now, in the evening, the windows are bright with displays of Limoges and other porcelain fit for the tables of princes, ramble on, dine and wine in a brasserie on the Grands Boulevards, finish up in the Folies Bergères, and come away bedazzled by a forest of lovely female legs taking sky-high kicks way beyond luscious breasts.

I shall spend the next five days doing the sights of Paris: the Louvre and the Musée d'Art Moderne. The view of the city rooftops from the Eiffel Tower and from the hill of Montmartre crowned by the white ice-cream cone of the Sacré Cœur church. The palaces and the parks. The Seine, its bridges, its quaysides with stalls of secondhand books and exotic birds and pet reptiles and dogs. The Notre Dame cathedral and the Latin Quarter, with which I fall in love.

I follow the long straight line of Rue de Rivoli onward across the breathtaking Place de la Concorde to the Champs-Élysées and the Arc de Triomphe. I linger in Rue des Rosiers, devoid of roses as befits a street imported from the *alte heim*, not that the gefilte fish I eat in a restaurant loud with Yiddish is cheap—it costs a *yakras*, a fortune. I take the underground Métro and emerge in a slum swarming with immigrants from the French colonies in Africa and Asia.

Do I neglect my midmorning rendezvous with the Yiddish literati? Oh, no! Religiously, every morning I stride down Magenta into Place de la République, an oblong so spacious I imagine it could accommodate a village with cows grazing in a meadow. A lofty monumental bronze dame brandishing in her right hand an olive sprig personifies the Republic. Below are more of her kind carved out of stone, and at the foot of the circular plinth a bronze lion stands guard over Liberty, Equality, and Fraternity.

On one side of the Place an enormous, grim building houses the Garde Républicaine, whose gorgeously uniformed horsemen adorn official state ceremonies.

Café Thénint is at the far end of the other side. There, instantly at home, I make fast friends with an elderly little poet and his essayist cousin. One morning, a large part of the Place is occupied by tens of thousands of leftists with banners in a mass rally celebrating the advent of the Popular Front government headed by a Socialist and Jew, Léon Blum. Slogans are chanted in support of the Frente Popular government in Spain, hard pressed by a fascist uprising of the regular army, its garrisons reinforced by troops from Morocco.

A refugee writer from Berlin foresees the triumph of Hitlerism throughout Europe and ultimately throughout the world. He says that the Frente Popular will be crushed under the weight of German arms, Stukka bombers, artillery, even poison gas, the works.

"But France under Léon Blum and his Front Populaire won't stand idly by," I object.

"That remains to be seen," he says. "Ever since the Allies, France and Britain, dictated the Versailles Treaty, they have reversed its provisions, disarming themselves and encouraging the rearmament of Germany. And now they look up to the Führer to pit the Third Reich against the Soviet Union. The democracies, so-called, much prefer anti-Semitic Nazism to supposedly Jewish Communism, as if Stalin who murdered Trotsky isn't a Jew hater. Mind you, Trotsky and Marx before him were self-hating Jews."

To this I cannot agree.

My good friend the poet, raising his soft voice to make himself heard above the tumultuous mass rally beside the bronze lion, gently dismisses the jeremiad with a wave of the hand over the emptied cups of black coffee: "We are not in the Dark Ages; forget the Spanish Inquisition. This is the twentieth century."

I cannot but heartily agree that this is the twentieth century. In the undoing of my education, sentimental and otherwise, I still have a long way to go.

An innocent in Paris, exultant and since the day before yesterday a smoker, I stock up with Gauloises cigarettes at a kiosk in the Gare du Nord before climbing three cast-iron steps into a third-class carriage of the Calais express.

29. THE RETURN TO LONDON AND MY RESOLUTION

My mind is made up; no more dithering. Fear of a storm of hysterics from my mother has kept me from telling her that I have decided to join the International Brigade serving with the Frente Popular forces in Spain.

I have been rehearsing for her benefit the imperatives of my decision so that she may see the light—a futile exercise, I know, because she won't listen. I foresee myself listening and listening and listening to her. I expect pleas of mercy; no, not for her sake but for mine. Will she not offer up prayers unto Elohim to bring me to my senses and not, Heaven forbid, risk life and limb in a war between savages and in a cause, a lost cause in the land of the Inquisition, that has nothing to do with me, Moishe? She may even break into English with "charity begins at home" and pick on Zion as the one proper place for me to scratch away at my itch for liberation, drenching the soil with my sweat, not my blood.

Braced to hear out her tirade, I shall keep my riposte *kurtz un sharf*, short and sharp: "The uncivil war raging in Spain marks the beginning of the war of Gog and Magog, the outcome of which will decide the fate of all mankind. And Elohim won't save me and you, and the Jewish pioneers in the Holy Land, and the people in the *alte heim*, if the Fascists triumph in Spain with the blessing of the Church and reinforced by arms and the help of troops from Hitler's Germany and Mussolini's Italy. It will be the beginning of a cataclysm, and if the so-called democracies, the hypocrites and stinkers, practice nonintervention, noninterference, it is for us the people to go to the rescue of the ship of humanism sinking in the Nazi mud!"

I know that I'll have said it all in an oversize nutshell to no effect. So one morning I blurt out a brief announcement of my intentions and get ready to listen and hold my tongue. But all I hear is—silence. I see the twitch between my mother's dark eyebrows spread to her whole face, to her shoulders, to her uplifted arms. This is not normal epilepsy—she doesn't have those fits any more—it's abnormal, it's creepy, it's ghastly, it's her dybbuk having himself a field day.

I wait for the frenzy to pass and then say, simply, "Mama, I'm not going to Spain."

I do and I don't fall back on my dreary routine. Outwardly I do so. Inwardly I fret. I loathe myself for my inertia. Each and every one of the International Brigade volunteers has a mother, except for the orphans. Mother or no mother, they're out there fighting. Some are dying or are maimed in action. Others, taken prisoner, are being tortured, executed. But so long as they're alive, they live. Do I live? No; I vegetate on behalf of charity at home.

In 1938, *The House of Napolitano* and *Jewish Short Stories of Today* are out on the bookstalls. Rich & Cowan, publishers of my novel, reports poor sales. The reviews are fine. Sean O'Faolain in the literary *John O'London's Weekly* writes: "If this is Martin Lea's first novel, he is something in the nature of a discovery. The novel has imprinted the name of the author on my mind. The next time I shall see it I shall read whatever he has written with the liveliest anticipation." This is just what the doctor ordered. But Sean O'Faolain will have to wait till doomsday to read my next book. There will be none.

There were, there still are, multiple reasons for my wanting to go to Spain—to get away from my mother Hindele, to do battle for the salvation of humanity, and above all to harvest raw material for a second novel. I aspire first and last to be a story writer, enriching reality with imagination, with dreams, with the insights of intuition. The prime need, of course, is experience of reality. And I have none, other than life with my mother and my father, which I must keep to myself. I'd sooner walk out stark naked into Lordship Park, a few houses off Queen Elizabeth Walk, than expose to public view my parents.

Frustrated and futile, I suffer onsets of depression, well camouflaged to escape my mother's notice. My previous vague notions of suicide mature into a definite and detailed plan. On one of my habitual shopping expeditions I shall walk out without any papers of identification in my pockets. I will cross the road in front of a speeding car, or why not a bus or a tram. The impact will hurt, but I'll be dead even before I can raise a scream in, to all appearances, one of the countless traffic accidents that happen every day. Hours will pass, I reckon, before I'm identified—hours in which my worrying mother will have got herself gradually, by degrees, into such a state of shock that the news of my demise will, as it were, be old hat. But then I picture to myself the horrific aftereffects. By treating myself to an easy death, I shall have condemned her to I know not what slow, agonizing, solitary death.

These fantasies, mental masturbations, serve to work off my depressions. I carry on with life from where I left off. Every now and then, àpropos of strictly nothing, I hear myself intoning that healing, Hasidic, neomessianic chant: "You know foon a goot plumber, en'it?!"

30. THE VISIT

The table in the parlor is laid with the porcelain tea set and with cheesecake and apple shtrudel in honor of A. M. Fuchs, the avant-garde Yiddish writer, come to visit my mother. And the blonde, slim girl accompanying him is his daughter Lola.

My mother settles him and herself in leather armchairs on either side of the couch that, hard up against the rear wall, is my bed at night. The chair I offer Lola she shifts away from the table. I place mine farther back and, from this vantage point, study the flow of her golden hair down to her slender shoulders.

Her father responds with an occasional nod to my mother's boisterous welcome. But on a mention of Shiya, he gravely recalls a visit from my uncle in Vienna. I know they are colleagues. Like I. J. Singer with his long short story *Perl*, A. M. Fuchs won instant acclaim with his novella *Oyfn Bergl* (*On the Hillock*) and was appointed Vienna correspondent of the *Jewish Daily Forward*.

I wince when my mother, singing my praises, mentions my anthology of Jewish short stories. A. M. Fuchs is not in it. *Oif'n Bergl* was too long for inclusion. And the several shorter pieces that came my way, portraits of the poorest of poor Jews amid the rich greenery of Galicia, were studded with uncommon, untranslatable Yiddish word combinations used to painterly effect. It would take a latter-day Bruegel to do them justice.

He shows no awareness of the anthology. Nor does his appearance betray his common stock with the wretched folk who people his writings. Of squat build, the stylish black suit he wears is certainly made to measure. And there is to his swarthy countenance with its beetling brows and mop of longish dark brown hair the air of a connoisseur rather than a creator of art, one who might fit a monocle in his eye before making a purchase. Unassuming, though, is what little he has to say in his homely Yiddish. And startling is the contrast between his heavy person and the fragility of his daughter sitting perfectly still in a distant, absent pose. It is she, not he, who arouses in me a quiver of curiosity.

The talk turns to the black plague of Nazism. My mother listens aghast to his tale of woe recounted in a matter-of-fact tone. After the Anschluss the family, first Lola and then he and his wife, were thrown into prison. After a couple of months they were released thanks to an American demarche at the prompting of the *Jewish Daily Forward*, which sent the family affidavits. On coming home they found two Gestapo officers who ordered them to pack two suitcases and instantly leave, but not before they signed an undertaking never to return.

When the train they caught at the Westbanhof crossed the Swiss border Fuchs threw the keys of their Vienna apartment out of the window and took a celebratory swig of slivovitz from the flat flask he'd tucked into an inner pocket.

In Paris they stayed awhile and then went on to London, where he has two brothers and a nonagenarian mother. Here they again ran into trouble. Lola's Austrian passport was made out in her maiden name, and she was accused of entry under false pretenses. An order was issued for her deportation to Honduras, and only after weeks of pleading was it rescinded.

My mother asks, "And where's Lola's husband?"

"Still in prison in Vienna."

My mother's horrified tics lapse into a fixity of calculation, followed by a bright proposal: "Morris, why not show Lola around London?"

"If Lola has nothing better to do," I say. I take her silence for acquiescence, and when I see our guests to the front door, in a few awkward words I make a date with Lola.

At night I lie on my couch picturing Lola. Lola on the now-empty chair in moonlight, Lola a prisoner in Vienna, Lola a deportee in red-light Honduras, Lola at my side when I'll take her out on Saturday. I also ponder what doesn't bear thinking of—my mother's scheme on hearing that girlish Lola was a married woman who might gratify but not run off with Mama's Moishele.

Have I fallen in love with Lola at first sight? In love, maybe, but not at first sight. I have yet to look Lola straight in the face.

31. LOLA

On Saturday, cloaked in my raglan overcoat—in disregard of the exceptionally mild weather for late autumn—I loiter in Carysfort Road, present myself a deliberate seven minutes late past two o'clock, and am admitted by a tall, black-haired matronly beauty out of a Russian romance. She calls Lola's father Fuchs, and he introduces her as Sonia.

When Lola appears in a silvery-gray, knee-length suit she takes quick leave of "Papa" and "Mutti"—speaking and spoken to in German. Mystified by the absence of any resemblance between herself and either of her parents, I follow her downstairs.

On the front seat of the upper deck of a bus, from which she may best view my London streets, I sit bolt upright—lest our shoulders touch in stop-and-start jolts. All too conscious of my gauche posture I venture sidelong glances. And in glimpses of her profile veiled by wavy golden hair I discern or imagine I discern suppressed laughter. At the Angel intersection, about to remark on the unangelic character of this and other crossroads in life, I have second thoughts. A witless witticism will do no good.

I take Lola to Bloomsbury and its literary landmarks, to the Strand and the Thames Embankment, then by bus to Marble Arch. We cross into Hyde Park and at the Speakers' Corner pause before a long-haired, red-nosed orator perched perilously on an upper rung of a stepladder. He whirls his arms up and down like a windmill caught in a to-and-fro gale.

In my halting German I tell Lola that his hoarse frenzy is in glory of the kingdom of heaven as opposed to the vanities of life on earth. The spirit moves me to flourish my right arm at Park Lane beyond the railings and my left arm at the Speakers' Corner. "Look," I say, "on the one hand, paradise on earth, the mansions of the idle rich, and on the other, the pride of British democracy, an open-air asylum for lunatic windbags."

Lola tilts her head back and favors me with a quizzical scrutiny. I return the gaze and do so without restraint. I behold the live model of a portrait I'd never seen before, yet nonetheless uncannily familiar. The pale, bloodless, oval face is set with wide-apart, wide-open blue-gray-emerald eyes with long dark lashes, arched by dark brows overhung by a stray golden lock. And in the whites of the eyes I see childish wonderment, but there is also also rueful mockery in the curve of the brows, the stray lock, the delicate flare of the nostrils, the set of the full mouth, and the stubborn little chin.

No longer a stranger is Lola, who wonders why the wonders of the world are decked in absurdity but not—as I regard it—steeped also in malice and deceit, in passions foul and monstrous. I resist the urge to take her by the elbow but say, "Come, we're going to be late for tea. It's a sin to miss teatime in England, much worse than skipping church."

I take her to the Lyons' Corner House temple. We ascend the broad staircase into brilliant light and soft music, wait for a couple of worshippers to rise from one of the thousand and one tables, are ministered to by a waitress vested in the sacramental apron tied into a bow at the back, are served the pot of tea for two I order, and are offered a trayload of cakes and pastries.

Happily for me, who is once again tongue-tied, Lola sits lost in thought. She nibbles a bit of Dundee cake and gently slides the plate with the leftover toward my plate emptied of a chocolate eclair. It is time to leave.

In the blaze of neon lights on Leicester Square I wonder how to prolong the afternoon. I read on a cinema facade the destination for which I'd been racking my brains: THE MARX BROTHERS.

Lola and I are both Marxists.

When I see Lola home I murmur: "Next Saturday?"

Whether or not her amused smile is prompted by my Harpo Marx–like solemnity, I read into it acceptance.

32. LOLA DESCRIBES THE ANSCHLUSS

I find occasion—Shakespeare at the Old Vic, ballet at the Sadler's Wells, an early black-and-white film—to celebrate with Lola the Sabbath two or even three times a week. The only time I take her arm is to help her in and out of rowboats on the river Lea. But there is between us a growing intimacy. She needs someone with whom to share her broodings on the upset in her life. Listening is my forte.

One evening, after a matinee, she recalls the Anschluss in a matter-of-fact tone of voice:

"I was sitting with friends in the Bauernstube—it's a semi-basement café, young people meet there—when the radio broke off martial music with a thunderous announcement: 'The Führer Adolf Hitler has entered Austria.' More martial music, followed at intervals by further announcements of Hitler's progress from town to town, sounding as if the Heavenly Father Himself had graced Linz . . . Graz . . . St. Polten . . . Wiener Neustadt . . . We sat in silence till he reached Vienna. Then we all scattered. A couple of Czech students said at the door they were going to cross the border at night on foot. It was the last I saw of my friends.

"I took the tram home, a ten-minute ride. My father was pacing up and down the living room, smoking a cigarette. 'Papa, haven't you heard the news, Hitler is in Vienna?' 'I am an Austrian citizen'—he shrugged—'and my papers are in order, taxes paid, no arrears.' 'All the same, shouldn't we pack up and leave?' He started to laugh."

I ask, "He laughed?"

"He guffawed and said, 'You're being childish!' He knew—I didn't—
that there was going to be a torchlight procession that night, and he
warned me to stay indoors.

"Early next morning I slipped out. Never before or since have I seen
such masses of people, multitudes flowing like lava to the Ring-
strasse—it's the grand boulevard encircling the Old City—and they
were all wearing the swastika pinned to their lapel. Vienna, you know,
had been a Social Democrat stronghold. But overnight they had re-
nounced their beliefs and were totally transformed.

"When I got to the Ring, skirting the Parliament, I wriggled my way
up front for a breath of air. On the other side are four rows of tall, age-
old chestnut trees; aloft in their branches hundreds of children, also
grown-ups, were waving swastika flags.

"From afar I heard a military march and a chorus of 'Heil, Hitler! Heil!
Heil!' The din rose till it was earsplitting. The brass band appeared, an
enormous band, followed by infantry in brown uniform, S.S. I suppose; next came the Gestapo in black; then black limousines.

"The parade passed on. For minutes on end there was breathless silence. A single limousine approached slowly, slowly, with an escort
of Gestapo on foot and on motorbikes. In the open Mercedes stood
Hitler, stiff like a waxen figure, his right arm upraised."

"You could," I say, "have shot and killed him."

"I could, if I had a gun and knew how to handle it. In the frenzy of adoration I was afraid the children dancing up in the chestnut trees were

going to fall off. At the tail end of the procession came more troops and more limousines, followed by thousands, tens of thousands, of worshippers. I was swept along to the Heldenplatz, Heroes' Square, of the Hofburg, the Imperial Palace. There, beside an equestrian statue, was a podium bedecked with swastika flags and with loudspeakers turned in all directions. Hitler mounted it, his right arm still upraised. And with him, all arms but mine upraised, his worshippers sang the Horst Wessel song.

"I went home, never told my parents where I'd been. A week later on Lichtensteinstrasse a man in civilian clothes stopped me. 'Fraulein,' he asked, 'are you Jewish?' I answered 'Yes!' He took me to Gestapo headquarters, ordered me to go down on my knees and scrub a spotless floor smelling of carbolic, and when he saw I wasn't much good at it, floundering in a puddle, he asked, 'Fraulein, shall I fetch you help?' 'I'll manage,' I said.

"A Black Maria took me away to the Elisabethpromenade prison. There I was interrogated, gave my name and the name and address of my parents, and was put into a narrow, bare cell crowded with eight women. We slept in our clothes on the wooden floor, a sloping floor, and when one of us turned over we all had to turn over, we were so cramped. The cell had nothing but a lavatory up against the back wall under a tiny window, and I was privileged to sit on its seat.

"Next morning we were served tepid brown water and nothing to eat. Then, while the cell was being cleaned, we stood outside on a gallery. And from a men's gallery below came my father's voice: 'Loli, where's Mutti?' He may not have heard me, but from the way I waved my arms, he could tell she wasn't with me.

"Our diet was a horrid broth with a stale piece of bread for lunch and what passed for coffee at supper. There was talk of our being sent to a concentration camp. 'No,' I said, keeping my spirits up on the lavatory seat. 'We shall be set free.' After three months, I—none of the others—was released. My father had received an affidavit from Ab Cahan, the editor of his New York paper *Der Vorwarts*. How did it reach him in prison? I don't know. At the sight of me he cried: *'Mein Gott, Loli, wie Du aussiehst!'* (My God Loli, how ghastly you look!) 'You don't look so wonderful yourself, Papa,' I answered.

"We went home. No sign of Mama. She was in the Landesgericht, a prison for long-term convicts. A few days later she joined us, saying: 'When the wardress called me out of the cell I didn't want to leave; I had settled in.'"

I order a second pot of tea for two in the Lyons' tea shop to which we'd repaired after the matinee performance of some tragedy or other.

33. THE CONFESSION I NEVER MADE

Unforgotten down the years and the decades is the flagstone on which I stop short when Lola on one of our outings asks, "Are you writing a second novel?"

"No," I say.

"Why not?"

"I have nothing to write about."

She gazes long and hard into my face.

Lola's English isn't yet up to reading *The House of Napolitano*, but she takes me on trust as a writer of promise and plainly takes to heart my retort of "nothing to write about." Having blurted it out I owe her an explanation.

In what could and should be a moment of truth I do not have it in me to confess to the kink in my makeup from early childhood onward. Burdened with my mother's tales of abuse by her own mother and traumatized by the sight and sound of her epileptic fits, all my reflexes are conditioned to never, ever hurting my sick mother, come what may. Yet I cannot forgive myself for not having gone off to fight in Spain, there to live my own life and, if need be, die. In self chastisement I sulk.

I do have a ready-made theme for a second novel—my own life thus far. But entwined as it is in the lives of my mother Hindele and my father Avrum, exposure is taboo.

I hold my tongue and feast on Lola's reminiscences rooted in love.

34. FUCHS AND SONIA

A young poet from a hill in Galicia goes to Warsaw, finds a publisher for his verse, and then works his passage to New York, there to seek his fortune. In a public library on Fifth Avenue he loses his heart to a lovely teenage brunette, an immigrant from Russia. He proposes to her—proposes elopement to Europe. Not to his fastidious taste is the crudity of the New World. She, although taken with his slim volume of poems, refuses to be torn away from her parents, her four sisters, and her one brother.

Adieu!

He works his passage to Hamburg—and from Hamburg straight back to New York. After the heartache of a three-week-long parting he, who now wears white kid gloves, presents himself anew to his sweetheart. He cannot live without her, but neither can he resign himself to the coarse American mode of life. Will she, will she not cross the Atlantic with him? She will.

On the voyage, working his passage, he accuses her, whose passage is paid, of flirting with the ship's officers dancing attendance on her. The pattern is set for his future paroxysms of jealousy.

Penniless in Vienna, the lovers lodge with a hospitable poet and essayist, Melech Ravich, who happily is also a bank clerk. Freethinkers, they nevertheless undergo a rabbinical marriage.

The poet A. M. Fuchs turns to prose—to a genre of storytelling all his own in style and substance. His tales are peopled by men and women who, alongside the beasts and the birds, the reptiles and the insects, are among the more obnoxious members of the animal kingdom. Flashes of fantasy illuminate the coarse realities of the everyday life depicted in his writings and into which he was born on a hillock in Galicia.

The couple are blessed with a daughter, Lola, who in time comes to learn of her parents' love story. On an emotional occasion the mother, Sonia, to ripples of laughter and with unshed tears glistening in her Russian black eyes, confesses to her daughter that it was the pair of white kid gloves sported by Fuchs on his return to New York that moved her to accept his suit.

I trace my genesis to a perverse maternal grandmother—and Lola hers to a white-kid-gloved hand that guides the pen into symphonies of the lowly human condition.

* * *

Another Anschluss takes place—the Sudetenland province of democratic multiracial Czechoslovakia is bestowed on the Führer Adolf Hitler courtesy of the prime ministers of Great Britain and France and the Italian Duce Benito Mussolini, gathered for the occasion in Munich. Neither the Czech government, nor the Soviet Union with which it has a precarious defense treaty, has been consulted. The unopposed annexation of the rest of the country by the Third Reich—sooner rather than later—is a foregone conclusion.

The British premier, Neville Chamberlain, on his return home from this, his third hasty pilgrimage to the Führer, triumphantly waves in his hand a copy of the surrender pact. Mouthing an assurance of "peace in our time," he is accorded a hero's welcome. The grin on the Right Hon. Gentleman's hawkish little face is unforced. He belongs to that common species of politician who goes through the motions of believing his own lies before he sells them to the public at large.

Winston Churchill equates Chamberlain's self-deceit with "a total and unmitigated defeat." Against the tide of appeasement of the expansionist Nazi tyranny Churchill depicts himself swimming "in the dark waters of despair."

What can a nonswimmer like myself do in a slough of despond? In retroactive wishful thinking the fancy takes me that the Academy of Fine Arts in Vienna, after twice closing the door on Adolf Schicklgruber, the would-be artist devoid of talent, at last bids him enter. He then settles down to make a career of sorts with his daubs, which he, of dubious paternity, may or may not sign "Hitler"—and all will be well! But on second thoughts this scenario doesn't hold water. In his stead another frustrated egomaniac is bound to arise, a rabble-rouser, a Führer catering to the frustrated dregs of humanity, transforming their inferiority complex into a magnificent sense of master race superiority.

If frustrations were amenable to psychotherapy . . . and if ifs and ands were pots and pans, there'd be no need for tinkers.

After Munich, what else can I do but go on from where I left off with my life?

35. LOLA IN VIENNA

I pursue my courtship of Lola. I love her the more for being unlike myself in all but one trait—a lingering childish wonderment at the world we live in, or rather the worlds apart that neither of us has outgrown. Uprooted from hers in the Nazi tempest, Lola remains high-spirited. I, a homebody, am dejected. We differ even in wonderment.

Ours is a meeting of opposites that dovetail—up to a point. Lola has a husband in Vienna, and I may never get to know her as "Adam knew Eve his wife." But containing my lust I crave to know all else there is to know of her. And I do believe she holds nothing back, eager to recapture her lost world.

Lola tells me of her first childhood memory—I ask for it. She stands sobbing in a meadow of the Prater, an amusement park in Vienna. She was playing hide-and-seek with her Papa, and she has lost sight of him. And oh, how she skips and hops for joy when he reappears from behind a tree!

On the strength of A. M. Fuchs's novellas and short stories I can well imagine how he, for his part, basks in the tenderness, the frailty, the delicacy of his daughter—nothing, but nothing, like those louts of his native Galician hillock, the mothers foulmouthed sluts and the fathers clumsy boors.

Papa Fuchs's delight is Mama Sonia's distress—an only child who refuses to eat and is nourished on Nestle's milk and cream.

Sonia, the statuesque black-eyed Russian beauty, is a seamstress plying the needle for groschens—till Fuchs is appointed the Vienna correspondent of the New York *Vorwärts* by Ab Cahan, patron of avant-garde Yiddish literature. She then puts her fingers to better use, taking piano lessons at the Theodor Lichetizsky school of pianoforte, of which Paderewski, among other virtuosi, was a student. Six-year-old Lola must also take lessons. But, says Theodor's widow, "The child can't sit still; she's a dancer. Take her to the Staatsoper ballet school."

Sonia does so. Lola is auditioned and accepted by the White Russian countess who runs the school. Mama sits watching the afternoon classes and, every Saturday, takes Lola to matinee performances at the Volksoper, the People's Opera House. Music is Sonia's passion.

Papa takes his Lola on outings to parks, to the zoo, to museums, and on excursions to the Schönbrunn Palace. He buys her picture books, even speaks to her of grown-up books but not of his own writings. Never a word does she hear of his Galician hillock. A wry jester, he indulges in quips that mystify her but make her laugh by their very tone. Gravely he intones *"Es hat mich sehr grefreut!"* (I was delighted!) after the manner of the erstwhile emperor of Austria and apostolic king of Hungary, bewhiskered Franz-Josef, whose exquisite courtesy withstood all bereavements: the execution of his brother Maximilian, emperor of Mexico; the suicide of his only son and heir, Rudolf; the murder of his wife Elizabeth by an anarchist; and the assassination of his nephew, the archduke Franz-Ferdinand, together with the archduchess, whose untimely demise in Sarajevo sparked off the Great War. This is Papa Fuchs's way of mourning and also ridiculing the charms of pre–World War I Vienna.

Fuchs's monthly salary, converted from dollars into inflated schillings, is better than that of the ministers in the republican government. Against the protests of Sonia, who is happy with their modest two rooms in a working-class neighborhood, he acquires on bourgeois Semperstrasse a spacious apartment with folding doors and five windows overlooking the street and the green grounds of the Rothschild hospital.

Before moving in, Fuchs has the new home renovated, from ornamented ceilings and candelabras to parquet floors. With a fine flair for decor he selects wallpaper of diverse pattern and coloring for each room, with Persian carpets to match. The salon is furnished in the Biedermeier walnut style, enhanced with a large antique Chinese vase. An oak desk, a tall, glass-fronted oak bookcase, a one-legged hexagonal table, and a pair of easy chairs upholstered in pigskin are installed in his study. A settee, two armchairs, and a wardrobe are placed in the L-shaped entrance hall. The bathroom is next to the maid's room. And Sonia is appeased with an Erhardt piano, on which she will play classical music day in, day out, for hours on end.

Lola starts elementary school. There the children laugh at her because she speaks only Yiddish. At home Fuchs clutches his head when he hears that she has to stand up for the Lord's Prayer. He and Sonia no longer speak Yiddish in Lola's presence. They send her to an expensive secular school and engage a governess, Helena, to teach her German.

Helena, behind the back of her profane employers, preaches religion and takes Lola to synagogue for pre-Sabbath prayers. Happily, every Friday the cloth draping the Ark is changed, and Lola is eager to see what color it will be this week. Unhappily, she is late for school every morning because Helena stops to flirt with the guardian of the clock tower on Schottentor Square. And when nudged, Helena hands out slaps.

Lola suffers in silence. Mama and Papa do not believe her when at last she tells. Nevertheless, Helena is replaced by Hilde, also Jewish but a strictly nonobservant intellectual, whose mother is the widow of a major in the Austrian army. Twelve years on, Hilde is gently asked to leave but chooses to stay on without wages. She and Lola are fast friends.

Sweet as life is in Vienna, it is sweeter still in the summer—two months spent on the island of Grado off Venice and the third month in Munchenkirchen, a village in the Alpine foothills.

Comes one summer when Fuchs and Sonia decide to go to a spa, Baden bei Wien, he for the sake of its Roman relics and she to pay homage to Beethoven, Mozart, Schubert, and Johann Strauss, who all lived and composed there. Having booked in at a hotel they set forth with Lola for their first—and last—stroll through the elegant town, to the Kurpark, where bejeweled ladies in finery and their gentleman escorts disport themselves or take their ease amid splashing fountains and mown lawns and flowerbeds and statues.

In all innocence Lola asks, "Where do we go from here?" Informed that they are come to stay for the whole summer, she bursts into tears, stamps her ballerina feet, declares she will run away—and away she runs. Sonia and Fuchs run after her, return to the hotel, pick up their luggage, pay the bill, and take Lola to Waldeck in the Alps, where the water splashes in streams, the grass grows thick, the flowers are wild, and the cows graze.

Fuchs is a staunch Socialist and Zionist. Lola therefore belongs to the Red Falcons, the Social Democrat Scouts, and to Hashomer Hatza'ir, the ultra-left Young Guard of the Zionist Movement. She dons its uniform—a blue blouse, a white scarf knotted to spread out into a triangle on the chest, a black skirt—and joins ten children in her age group.

On Saturday mornings the many companies of ten, each led by a senior Young Guard, set out on a hike by as many different itineraries to a given meeting place far out in the country. There they hear lectures, eat lunch from their satchels, and either do or do not drink bottled water. Especially after a stiff climb in hot weather, gaunt and bristly Reuven, the company leader, deems it proper to accustom his charges to the thirst that awaits them in arid Zion. So be it! The children sing and dance the hora, flirt, fall in and out of love, sit around a campfire at night, hear more lectures, again sing in chorus, and boisterously return to the hushed city.

Lola now spends part of the summer holidays with Hashomer Hatza'ir. On an excursion to Split in Yugoslavia she is desperately enamored of a gifted young writer, a non-Jew, come to report on a visit he has paid to the Soviet Union. He will be executed on the morrow of the Anschluss. She is also secretly in love with a Hashomer Hatza'ir senior, whom she will mourn after he dies fighting in Spain.

In the Hashomer Hatza'ir club, a large upper floor with a rooftop garden on Wahringerstrasse, Lola is pestered by unsuitable suitors who insist on seeing her home of an evening. Among them are a pair of redheads, twin brothers, one of whom carries a switch to lash out at her legs.

At fourteen Lola quits classical ballet at the State Opera for the elite Gertrud Kraus modern dance troupe. It is expressionist, pulsating with the rhythm, the turbulence, of real life. Its only other exponent worldwide is Mary Wigman. Gertrud Kraus takes to Lola, calls her Lolita, and has her play second-lead parts in performances at the Konzerthaus.

On occasion Lola, preparing for matriculation, skips school to avoid the torment of the math lesson. One sunny morning, engrossed in her best-loved author, Thomas Mann, she is joined on a park bench by a well-mannered young man who ventures to ask what she is reading. It's *Der Zauberberg—The Magic Mountain*. He wonders if she has read Jakob Wassermann, who is his uncle. He further introduces himself as a newly qualified doctor who, with dark forebodings of the near future in Europe, intends to practice in America.

Uninvited he turns up in Semperstrasse and addresses to Fuchs, who has a nodding acquaintance with Jakob Wassermann, a proposal of marriage to Lola. For all his refinement, he does not wear white kid gloves and must leave for New York without her.

Dare I at this point ask to whom she is married? I dare. Lola answers. Among her circle of friends, dancers, and theater professionals is a newcomer from Berlin, Ernst Ehrenfeld. He is a photographer without a camera. His mother, a film actress, has no use for a very tall, exceptionally handsome son who gives her age away. His father, a film producer and director, is at her beck and call. Ernst is a penniless refugee from his wealthy parents, one of whom—he does not say who—is Jewish but unmolested by the Nazis.

In Vienna Ernst can have his pick of mistresses. High-society ladies seek him out to be photographed. He borrows a camera, is offered the use of a studio, and the ladies depart with nothing more romantic than portraits of themselves.

Whenever he pockets a fat fee he takes Lola out to expensive restaurants and nightclubs. When stony broke, which is most of the time, he sees her home in the small hours, and she tosses out of a third-floor window the supper Sonia has laid out for her.

On such nights the house porter, who locks the portal at midnight, is roused from his sleep. One day he puts in a discreet word: *"Herr Fuchs, ich wurde auf Fraulein Lola ein bisschen mehr Acht geben!"* (Herr Fuchs, in your place I'd take a bit more care of Fraulein Lola!) His advice is as gracious as it is gratuitous. Fuchs has long since been shadowing Fraulein Lola, the while deeming paternal silence the better part of discretion. But one day he speaks up and blunders: "Your Don Juan will pocket you and your pocket money, but he'll never marry you!"

"Oh, no?" says Lola, who of late has cooled toward Ernst, the playboy, who has taken to hobnobbing with a young Nazi.

The wedding she did not contemplate is celebrated in the Grand Synagogue in the Old City and duly attended by her parents. She goes on living with them, since her husband has no fixed address, lodging with friends here and there.

A few weeks later Vienna hails Hitler. Lola and her parents spend three months in jail. Released and under an expulsion order, she goes looking for Ernst—he is nowhere to be found. Two black-uniformed Gestapo men take possession of the third-floor apartment in 29 Semperstrasse. Permitted under close observation to pack all of two suitcases, Fuchs, Sonia, and Lola then sign an undertaking never to return to Ostland.

On a Paris-bound train, past the frontier into Switzerland, Fuchs flings out of the carriage window the Semperstrasse keys that spell homelessness and celebrates with a swig of slivovitz freedom regained.

36. LOLA IN PARIS

Aglitter with marble—such is Paris, *la ville lumière*, the City of Light, in Lola's imagination.

Stepping out of the Gare de l'Est, Fuchs flourishes at a taxi driver the address of a Jewish-owned hotel. It's an elegant, three-star establishment on the corner of a boulevard. From her divan by the window in the room Lola shares with her parents she looks out on an ill-lit cobblestone alley. A prostitute posted at a lamppost is being teased by a policeman, who backs off into a doorway whenever a passerby stops to look the lady over. The scene would have been an ideal curtain raiser to a pas de deux staged by Gertrud Kraus in the Konzerthaus. No, the past must be forgotten; the black plague of Nazism has engulfed Vienna. The scene now is Paris and is awaiting the brush of one or another of the three thousand painters gathered from far and near in the capital of art.

Reality soon overtakes imagination. The editor of *Die Neie Presse*, which carries a front-page report of A. M. Fuchs's arrival, has set up a rendez-vous with an "up and coming" painter from a shtetl in Lithuania, in the Cafe Thénint on Place de la République. He turns up late. An unshaven dandy with a slick of brilliantined black hair all but covering one dark eye, he has the feverish air of a Jew on the run. His handshake is loose, uneasy. Lola and Sonia, whom he ignores, pay scant attention to what he in his clipped Litvak Yiddish and Fuchs in his broad Galician accent have to say to each other. When he fumbles in his wallet to pay the wait-er for the repeated espressos, Sonia prods a heel into Fuchs's trouser leg under the table, not that he needs a signal to play the host. The parting is slow. The feverish Litvak wants Fuchs to come and see his paintings—his studio isn't far off. The invitation is declined with hemming and hawing excuses. So ends the encounter with Chaim Soutine.

Soutine? Did I not hear that same name mentioned many years later when I sat with the sweet Yiddish poet and his stern cousin, the essay-ist, on the terrace of the Cafe Thénint on sunny Place de la République exulting in the Front Populaire and the Frente Popular? In years to come I shall take cold comfort in the thought that, even had I then made Chaim Soutine's acquaintance and seen his paintings—and why not also have bought a canvas for a song?—I'd have been unfit to appreciate his unique creations that, innocent of Matisse beauty, of Picasso boldness, of Chagall fantasy, alone capture the rock-bottom re-ality of the 20th century. With the doomsday foresight of the Hebrew prophets, the hounded Litvak Soutine depicted the forthcoming degra-dation of humanity into the foulest of all animal species.

His *Plucked Chicken*, replete with arms and legs and beak, nay, mouth wide open in a last cry of agony, foretells the Holocaust. His land-scapes are swept by nuclear blasts. The *Groom* in gaudy uniform, arms akimbo, thighs outspread wide from his genitals, face drawn into pert solemnity, is a study in utter inanity—the prerequisite of monstrosi-ties all down the ages.

Lest Lola go astray in Paris, Fuchs gets a young reporter of *Die Neie Presse* to show her around town. Prim, proper, a bore, he takes the edge off sightseeing. She gives him the slip.

In the Louvre, amid the grave knot of tourists contemplating a certain smile, Lola is addressed in German by a stranger: "Fraulein, how do you like the *Mona Lisa?*"

A middle-aged gentleman, who likes her smile, introduces himself as an artist and a writer from London and offers to escort her to an Egon Schiele exhibition.

The name *Schiele* is familiar—it spells Vienna. The paintings are a revelation—skeletal nudes, bloodless except for elbows and knees flushed scarlet.

Lola's newfound companion takes her to the Latin Quarter. When crossing the Pont Neuf, he stops to gaze down at the Seine and tells her of the trouble he has with the ending of the novel he's writing. Its protagonist on this very same bridge plunks down a briefcase containing the manuscript of his memoirs, vaults over the parapet, and drowns. That melodramatic finale won't do, and he can't think of anything better. "Why not," says Lola, "have the suicidal character toss his memoirs into the river and just walk away?"

Companionship warms into friendship. There are more rendezvous. He takes her to a villa on the outskirts where *le tout Paris* is assembled to hear Wanda Landowska on the harpsichord.

Will Lola, he asks, pose for him—no, not in the nude—in the atelier of a fellow artist? She will. After she has sat still two full days, he shows her the finished painting. The dreamy eyes are blue. For the rest, she sees herself portrayed in a near-transparent white cloud touched with sunshine. The strongest tint is her hair. She regrets having varnished her fingernails.

Astonished, she thanks him for the presentation, which she will be happy to accept as soon as the oils are dry. Amused, he tells her he intends to keep it, but that is no reason why she should not thank him, truly thank him. She steps up to him, plants a kiss on one cheek, and retreats. He stands bemused but collects himself. Will she go and have dinner with him? She will.

He takes her to a nightclub, Le Sphinx. The bare-breasted waitresses serve delicious dishes and their delectable selves to diners disposed to follow them up a flight of stairs. Lola offers to wait for her portraitist, if he wishes to go up. He does not so wish. Done eating, he sees her into a taxi and waves adieu.

No more adventures for Lola. She returns to the Louvre with her parents. In front of a barefooted *David*, Sonia remarks on the sore red toes of the weary shepherd boy. Evenings are spent in Montparnasse at the cafés frequented by artists, Le Dome, La Coupole, La Rotonde. They meet Mane-Katz, the joyous painter of the *alte heim*. "Fuchs," he says in Yiddish, pointing at Lola, "is this your doing?"

Lola is impatient to get away. In Vienna she gave the London address of Fuchs's elder brother, Shiya, to a Gentile girl friend who promised to write, if and when there was news of Ernst Ehrenfeld.

37. LOLA IN LONDON

"London won't run away," says Fuchs, in no hurry to leave Paris.

Lola runs away. She travels on the passport her father obtained in her maiden name.

Journey's end is a red-brick dwelling in an outlandish cluster of red-brick dwellings called Bethnal Green. Red bricks belong on factory walls where Lola belongs, in Vienna.

In her handbag she has no English currency for the taxi fare. Shiya pays. He then hugs and kisses his niece, whom he has never seen before, and puts a phone call through to the Paris hotel to announce her unannounced safe arrival.

After being hugged and kissed by her aunt Annie and her three cousins—handsome Cyril and Harold studying medicine at Cambridge, and teenage Lily—Lola is taken to an upstairs room where, attended by a nurse, lies her grandmother. When finally she manages to understand what she is being told, that at her bedside stands Avremele's daughter, she catches her breath for a whisper: *"A sheine!"* A beauty.

Another affectionate uncle, frail, mousy-complexioned Suma, puts in an appearance. Editor of a giveaway Yiddish journal crammed with his own unpretentious writings signed "Lisky," he lives off Shiya's largesse. The three Fuchs brothers from the Galician hillock dearly love but in no way resemble one another. Robust Shiya is fair, curly-headed, blue-eyed, and jovial. A tinsmith employing hired workers in the basement, he has made his fortune turning out kettles under contract to the British army.

Lola shares a bedroom with Lily, who is torn between two desires: marriage or a career as a schoolmistress. "Do both; marry *and* be a schoolmistress," says Lola, adept at solving dilemmas—if not her own, then that of others. Lily will become a headmistress and the wife of a part-time cantor who profitably plays the stock exchange with his rich dowry.

For Avremele and Sonia, Shiya sets aside in one of the several houses he owns a flatlet in Carysfort Road and offers to train his refugee brother in the fine art of kettle making. A. M. Fuchs knows better than to take offense and dispenses to his Bethnal Green kith and kin the gold-nibbed fountain pens and valuable trinkets he had, for that very purpose, stealthily tucked into his pocket when taking leave of the Gestapo in Semperstrasse.

Lola receives from her Gentile girlfriend in Vienna a letter from Ernst. Released from the Landesgericht prison, he is anxious to rejoin his wife. Necessary for immigration is a certified undertaking of his full maintenance by a well-established British citizen.

Lola procures the necessary printed form and asks Shiya to sign. He consults Avremele, who will not hear of it. In vain she tries to strike a bargain with her father—as soon as Ernst reaches London she will divorce him. Sulks and tantrums are to no avail with Shiya. When she declares she'll set the red-brick house on fire, he smiles.

Seated beside her aunt Annie and her cousin Lily in the women's gallery of a synagogue on Yom Kippur eve, Lola cannot help weeping all through the Kol Nidre service. She spends the next day alone and stays away from the supper that breaks the fast.

The exchange of correspondence with Ernst peters out. He stops writing. And she weeps no more—till she takes her place at the long table magnificently laid for the Passover seder. Absent are Fuchs and Sonia, but in attendance are Aunt Annie's four sisters, their husbands, and a gorgeous, pale-faced, dark-eyed niece who insists on sitting on her papa's lap. A knock is heard, then eerily another and another and another at intervals down the stairs. The door opens. In creeps a wraith. At the sight of her grandmother, Lola bursts into sobs, runs from the room, and nothing can entice her to come back.

She will cry no more when Fuchs, who, without her knowledge, has been in correspondence with the rabbinate in Vienna, tells of ways and means available for obtaining Ernst Ehrenfeld's safe conduct to Italy and thence to Switzerland on the proviso that she agree, as Ernst has done, to a divorce performed in two synagogues—the one in Vienna and the other in London.

Lola walks seven times round a Holy Ark, throws an empty wine glass onto the floor, splinters it underfoot, repeats incomprehensible Hebrew words, and is pronounced a *groosha*, a divorcee.

A few years later in Paris, on Boulevard Montparnasse, Lola will point at Ernst Ehrenfeld, who starts at the sight of her and me and walks past in silence.

38. START OF THE WAR

The Ecclesiastes dictum of nothing new under the sun holds good on one count and one only: the constancy of change in human affairs. Whether we regard it as progress toward the millennium or regress toward self-annihilation, or neither the one nor the other, its flow has never been broken since Adam took that forbidden bite on the apple of the tree of knowledge of good and evil.

"Peace in our time" having lasted all of eleven months plus two days, Britain is once more at war. So what's new? Like none other, this is a phony war. The French call it a *drôle de guerre*. With all due respect to Gallic wit, this war will be anything but droll.

There is to change another aspect of continuity: a procession of variations on familiar themes both big and little, epic and absurd. This being so, I make bold to trace the origins of the phony war to a recurrent frame of mind. I refer, if you please, to the persuasion that moved dear Shosha, our Lordship Park landlady, to accost the postman at the front door with: "You know foon a goot plumber, en't it!?" In the event, the plumber of her dreams did fix the leak, which wetted and threatened to bring down the ceiling in her kitchen.

Alas, the plumber designated by Neville Chamberlain and his ministers to dispel their nightmarish fears of Communist infiltration worldwide saw fit to thumb his nose at his would-be employers. In the person of Adolf Hitler alias Schicklgruber he went on to conclude a pact of "nonaggression and neutrality" with his sworn enemy, Joseph Stalin alias Dzugashvili, for the partition of Poland between the Third Reich and the Soviet Union. Whereupon Britain and France declared war on the Führer, doing so in righteous indignation after having paid him a hefty deposit—the surrender of Czechoslovakia following the Anschluss of Austria—for his hoped-for assault on the Bolsheviks.

In London up go the blackout curtains and down go the park railings to be melted into armaments, of which Great Britain is woefully short. Public air-raid shelters are installed for eventual use. The sirens are tested and found not wanting. Their funereal wail stirs in me a yen for the good old street crier's chant: "Take cover!" But change is the order of the day; there's no withholding the march of civilization.

The Wehrmacht, armed to the teeth in contravention of the Versailles Treaty with the blessing of the Western democracies, soon overcomes dogged Polish resistance. The Red Army does likewise. Britain, defaulting on its pledge of military assistance, offers Poland heartfelt condolences. The French take cover behind the Maginot Line.

As war casualties go, I have little cause for complaint. I am engaged by *The Daily Telegraph* of Fleet Street to monitor the German and French broadcasts and condense for publication the big lies of the Goebbels propaganda machine and the fanfaronades of la belle France.

Lola, however, is dispirited. Our roles have been reversed, and it has become my hallowed duty to try and cheer her up. Papa Fuchs, who has been interned on the Isle of Man in a camp for enemy aliens, is better at it than I am. His humorous letters tell of his daylong chore peeling potatoes and how he was taken aback when a fellow enemy alien exclaimed, "This is my watch you're wearing! Herr Fuchs, don't you recognise me? I'm Herr Waksel, the watchmaker on the Wahringerstrasse!"

I make love to Lola. We are lovers—this I tell myself, I do not declare it to her—lovers until death do us part.

39. THE WEDDING

Lola is pregnant. I should have taken precautions, waited for the nuptials. She has not told her parents—Fuchs is back from the Isle of Man—and she resists my attempts to plan our future. Marriage? I take her silence for acquiescence. I'm not at all sure she shares my pride and joy. We are, of course, two very different beings. I couldn't love her as I do if she were one of a kind with me. I know myself for what I am.

I must break the glad tidings to my mother but keep putting it off for tomorrow. There is no tomorrow. The sun sets and rises on today. And today trails behind me a burden of yesterdays—so many strings, my mother's convulsions, to which I jerk like a puppet. Not that I will submit to them; no, not this time, as I did when she stopped me from going off to see action in Spain.

The days lengthen into weeks. One night I find my mother waiting up for me. She greets me with a huge, mocking "Mazal Tov!," transforming my pride and joy into instant shame and vexation. Lisky, Lola's uncle, has informed the novelist Esther Kreitman of her son's clandestine liaison. The wee bulge in Lola's figure gave us away.

"Why," my mother cries, "why did I have to hear this from Lisky and not from you?"

"I was going to speak to you."

"Moishele was going to . . ."

The scene passes off without convulsions.

* * *

Lola and I are wed in the Stoke Newington Town Hall. The ceremony is graced by the *belle tournure* of the bride in a white-dotted pink crepe-de-chine dress, a white-dotted blue sash, a matching band on her golden hair, carnations in one hand, and onto the fourth finger of her left hand I slip a golden ring.

In attendance are our parents. We all wine and dine in a local restaurant. To farewell hand-waves I take Lola by the arm and away we walk—the long stroll in the sunshine will make do for a honeymoon—to the furnished flatlet I have rented in Seven Sisters Road facing Finsbury Park.

Early next morning, Lola and I are asleep. There's a ring at the door. It's my mother. "Go back to bed; don't mind me," she says, seating herself on the edge of the bed and then lying down beside me. I edge away, gritting my teeth at her deliberate insinuation of incestuous inclinations—there are none, there never has been the slightest hint of any—between Mama and her Moishele.

Lola hops out of bed, slips on a dressing gown, and performs an act she will later admit to having never attempted before—she cooks up a breakfast.

At table, my mother complains that the Hochdeutsch as spoken by Lola grates on her ears. Lola has never had much to say when my mother was around. Now and ever after she is silent in her mother-in-law's presence.

I do not protest. I only squirm.

* * *

Lola and I never miss an evening at the cinema or at the theater. Saturdays, my day off—the *Telegraph* doesn't appear on Sunday—we visit museums or go on excursions. We are seldom at home for a ring at the door. But on my way to or from work I make sure to drop in at Lordship Park and pay my filial respects.

The faraway war goes from bad to worse and draws closer. The Red Army has battered Finland into capitulation. The Wehrmacht overruns Norway and Denmark, then Holland and Belgium. Ahead of the fall of France, the Royal Navy evacuates the British Expeditionary Force from Dunkirk.

Winston Churchill in his first address as prime minister to the House of Commons warns: "I have nothing to offer but blood, toil, tears, and sweat." He also offers the promise of "Victory—victory at all costs, victory in spite of all terror; victory, however long and hard the road may be."

In the Duce's belief that the Führer has won the war, Italy joins the fray. American isolationist policy is tempered by Roosevelt with "all aid short of war" to Britain, bracing itself for invasion by the Third Reich. The BBC broadcasts warrior-poet Churchill's ode to the nation: "We shall fight on the beaches, we shall fight on the landing grounds, we shall fight in the hills, we shall never surrender . . ."

There is no more phony war. The sirens in London find their voice again—in earnest. Bombs rain down in broad daylight, but not for long. The Luftwaffe, having suffered heavy losses, now prefers to unload death and destruction under cover of darkness.

Lola is in her ninth month of pregnancy. The Civil Defence recommends an address in Hampton Court ready to receive her as an evacuee. Sonia escorts Lola and stays on, renting a nearby furnished room.

On Saturday I join Lola. All is peaceful in the large, timeworn house on Palace Road, chock-a-block with generations-old furniture and hung with Gospel lithographs. Large, timeworn Mrs. Card treats her five pregnant guests, two of them Jewish, with utmost unfussy consideration. Lola's heavily accented English enlivens the small talk. Withdrawn in a corner sits Sonia, statuesque.

Lola conducts me on the stroll she has daily been taking with her mother. We cross the Thames. Unruffled flow its waters, little knowing to what man-made thunder and lightning they are headed at nightfall. We pick our way through the Hampton Court maze, we roam the grounds, we gaze at the palace—open to the public, but we prefer to rest on a bench—and I brief Lola on Henry VIII's seven wives and their misfortunes.

Lighthearted, I return to Seven Sisters Road and there sleep soundly through the blitz.

Next Saturday I'm back in Palace Road. On leave from the Royal Navy, in civilian clothing, is the Cards' only son. Jovial and talkative, he has nothing to say about war and warships. But from a remark dropped by his father I infer that the large, weatherbeaten lad has seen active service in commando raids. I come away with the newfound, or rather the renewed, conviction that humanism will prevail over bestiality and that I have been getting my values all wrong.

In the meantime I imagine the wording of the message I shall be receiving in Lordship Park—I have no phone in Seven Sisters Road—from the Palace Maternity Home: "Mother and —— child are doing well." The gap is for a "boy" or a "girl."

On the twenty-second of September Lola is the mother and I am the father of a daughter, whom we shall name after her great-grandmother Hannah Temela Singer. Great indeed, she traveled the length and breadth of the *alte heim*, a purveyor of antique jewelry in high society, and at a ripe old age traveled to Jerusalem, a lone pilgrim, leaving her husband, the homebody rabbi, behind in the Galut, in exile. But even as I, Moshe, am Mozes on my Antwerp birth certificate and have since become Morris, so shall newborn Hannah be Hazel. Better still, Hazel Rhoda, because Lola also has a great-grandmother. Acculturation.

Impatiently I await notification of the day on which Lola and Hazel will be ready to leave the maternity home. I shall then bring a perambulator—the navy blue four-wheeler I have bought at the Army & Navy Stores deserves better than to be called a pram.

On my habitual evening call, I turn the key in the front door lock of 56 Lordship Park, step into the hall, and stop short. From the kitchen I hear my mother's voice in the distinctive didactic, querulous tone she has adopted for Lola.

I enter, beset with hallucinatory premonitions, happily dispelled. Lola sits, head bowed, over a crib of sorts, a basket. In it, rosy-faced and sound asleep, lies Hazel. I bend down and stir the coverlet. I know I shouldn't be waking the baby, but like all living creatures on earth who do what they shouldn't do, I can't help myself.

Hazel opens wide in wonderment wondrous blue eyes. In what may be no more than an instant but is timeless, her wonderment blends with mirthful recognition of the stranger stooping over her. I witness mystery devoid of fantasy.

I turn to Lola. Stony-faced, she has not budged from her chair. I want to hug and kiss her. I also want to rave and rant at her. Whatever unpleasantness may have arisen in Hampton Court—and I have a fertile imagination for distress—she should not have come here for more discomfiture at risk of life and limb.

The blackout curtains are drawn. My mother, her tics stretched into smiles, serves a lavish hot supper.

The sirens wail. Lola picks up Hazel and goes into the front room. I follow with the crib but insist: "We can't sleep here." She gives me a dismissive nod and turns away to breastfeed the baby.

We are the last down in the cellar. Cleared of coals and debris, if not of rats, it is become a regular dormitory crammed with camp beds for Shosha and all her tenants. My father points to a camp bed for Lola and another for myself. I shift them so that we lie side by side. There is little talk between the booms, the thuds, the crashes. I ask Lola, "What made you come to London?" I see—I can't hear—her laughter.

Snatches of sleep between nightmarish waking spells leave me dazed.

After breakfast I phone the *Telegraph* news editor. He wishes me to put off my departure till he can find someone to fill in for me. I consent.

Two days later I take my wife and child back to Hampton Court. There I will thrash matters out with Lola. On the short train ride she is unresponsive, gazing out of the carriage window.

From the station we walk to Palace Road. Mrs. Card and the expectant mothers, bemused with expectancy, give Hazel a rapturous welcome. The hours pass with Lola in high spirits—overly high spirits wrestling with melancholy and exhaustion.

Will Mrs. Card be kind enough to accommodate me overnight on a couch? No, not on a couch but in her sailor son's bedroom. Straight after supper I carry up a cot. Lola breastfeeds Hazel, undresses, and goes to bed.

I sit beside her and repeat the question I asked in the cellar: "What made you come to London?"

Again she laughs.

"You, my dear husband, sent your father to fetch me."

"I sent my father? If you can believe that . . . !? But tell me just what happened."

"What is there to tell? Some other time; I'm tired."

Lola closes her eyes. After a while, in a reverie, she recalls her first birth pang. She paid no heed to it, but Sonia knew better and called an ambulance. In the delivery room she labored from early evening all through the night into morning. The pangs became more and more excruciating till at last she truly wished herself dead—and then was delivered of new life. She heard its cry in a quietude more absolute than her worst spasms. She asked to see her child, only to see it whisked away. "A baby girl," said the nurse, who came to mop up the blood. "A beauty!"

Borne on a stretcher to a room shared with three other mothers, Lola raised a laugh in an outburst of plain English: "Did you hear me scream?" Later, when Hazel was brought in, rosy and without a wrinkle, blue-eyed and with a tuft of golden hair, one of the three mothers, whose baby was dark, furiously scarlet, and wrinkled, looked the other way.

"Now tell me about my father."

"There's nothing much to tell. I was in the maternity home, dressed, waiting for you to come and see the baby and take us to Mrs. Card. In came your father to take us away to London. I wanted to go and say good-bye to my mother or have her come with us, but he wouldn't hear of it."

"Your mother wouldn't have let him take you away."

"I wonder where she can be now. I simply did what your father told me to do."

"You simply? . . ."

"You simply don't understand. Try to understand. Your father is a stranger. The world is full of strangers, has been ever since the radio in the Bauernstube café blared 'Hitler has entered Vienna.' The mob who hailed him, swapping the three Social Democrat arrows for the swastika, weren't the civilized, happy-go-lucky *gemütliche* people among whom I'd grown up, not any more. They were perfect strangers. When a stranger on the Wahringerstrasse told me to go and scrub a Gestapo floor because I was Jewish, I went and scrubbed a Gestapo floor. When a stranger in Woburn House caring for Jewish refugees told me I was to be deported to Honduras because my passport was in my maiden name, to Honduras I'd have gone. But my uncle Shiya, who knows how to make kettles, also knows how to talk to strangers. So here I am. Your father is a stranger. If you didn't send him, then your mother did. She's a stranger."

"And I, their son, am a stranger."

"You're strange, but not a stranger from the very beginning. When Fuchs first took me along to pay his respects to Singer's sister, I saw how your mother had you at her beck and call. She graciously took it upon herself to suggest you act the cavalier to me, a married woman who might satisfy her poor boy's needs but not take him away from his mama. I felt sorry for you."

"And you took it upon yourself to save me, not knowing what you were letting yourself in for. But I knew and I am to blame. I have a sick, lonely, compulsive mother. Maybe eagerness to see her grandchild got the better of her."

"So very eager, she never cradled, never once touched, her grand-daughter, excusing herself by saying she had a bad cold. And she never once let me out of the house, never set down a glass of milk for me, but did open a tin of sardines and the next day a tin of pink salmon. Which is as much as one can expect of a stranger."

"You have asked me to try and understand. Believe me, Lola, I now do understand. Let's go to sleep."

"Before you turn off the light, let's look at all those pictures on the wall."

"Which, the racehorses or the nudes?"

"You look at the nudes. I'll look at the horses. I'd love to ride that black one with the white ankles."

"So, I guess, would that sailor over there, dreaming of it out at sea."

During the night Lola prods me awake. I was screaming in my sleep but, happily, didn't disturb Hazel.

I leave early in the morning. Lola sees me to the front door. I raise my arms for a reconciliation embrace. We kiss.

40. THE BLITZ

At night, I do part-time fire-watching on the rooftop of *The Daily Telegraph*. To hand are press-button fire extinguishers. The occasion to use them doesn't arise. A Wren church, St. Bride's, goes up in flames, but no other building in Fleet Street is struck in the blitz.

It is my modest lot to monitor what others say and do. The sinister German and abject Vichyite French broadcasts get under my skin. Outrage for outrage, the bombardment, at least, is impersonal.

The incendiaries burst like gigantic eggs spurting rotten yolks. The high explosives throw up clouds of dust and debris with or without shattered flesh and bones and spilled blood. Swaths and pools of the metropolis are burning. The heavenly rain of hellfire engenders the deceptive appearance of thunderous earth tremors with countless eruptions of lava. The dome of St. Paul's Cathedral shimmers as if rapt in prayer against the sickly yellow of the sky. In the absence of visible signs of life down below where Fleet Street runs into Ludgate Circus, nature—not mankind—seems to have gone berserk.

At daybreak while the conflagration is still raging and the salvage teams go on digging up the dead and the maimed, the uninjured millions of men, women, and children will emerge from the underground shelters to carry on with their lives as best they can. They have experienced discomfort and bereavement, but far from suffering humiliation, they know they have defied the enemy.

I can count myself lucky on a Fleet Street rooftop. Far better the risk of being blown to pieces than the certainty of being spat upon as a Jew.

Fire-watching on alternate Saturdays and the shrinking daylight hours in autumn and winter keep me away from Hampton Court. On my leisure Saturdays I cannot again ask for overnight accommodation. So in

Thames Ditton I rent a furnished room from a white-haired widow in want of companionship. Soon Lola is able to hold fluent conversation in quaint English. Wheeling Hazel in the pram, we take riverside strolls and go into Surbiton for tea. These Saturday and Sunday mornings before I catch a bus back to London are among the happiest in my life.

I sense exasperation in the repetitious German threats of an invasion of Britain. Together with the rough waters of the English Channel, the Churchillian strain in the British spirit holds Hitler at bay. He hurls the Wehrmacht at the Soviet Union.

I move from the *Daily Telegraph* to the Reuters news agency a few doors away. There I join a monitor of Moscow Radio. A spare, swarthy, curt-mannered man—a Jew, I guess, maybe twice my age—he and I become instant fast friends after an exchange of names; his is David Magarshack. Nothing am I going to learn of his antecedents, nor he of mine, in the three years we shall sit together exchanging refrains between broadcasts. He will harp on injustice—the injustice wreaked on the Russian classics by English translators turning plain language into pretentious phraseology. His heart goes out in particular to Dostoyevsky, who would turn in his grave if he could see how his down-to-earth expressions have been travestied. Never does Magarshack drop a hint of his own versions on which he is working and which I'll read in due time with relish. He will not read the original novels I plan, because I will never write them.

The blitz is over. I rent a ground-floor flat in a house on Canfield Gardens, whose absentee landlord is the film actor James Coburn. I furnish it with bare necessities. At long last Lola, Hazel, and I have a home of our own.

Magarshack often comes to have tea with us in the garden, which has two pear trees and half a cherry tree—the other half overhangs the neighbor's garden—and he gives them a hefty shaking to take back fruit to his ailing wife in Hampstead.

My mother—seldom my father—also comes visiting. Long-suffering, her mood is subdued. In my spare time I have set about translating *Der Shaidim Tantz—Dance of the Demons*—which will see print retitled *Deborah*. She has since written a second novel, *Brillianten Diamonds*, in which our one-time kind host Yakobovich, the ritual slaughterer, is transfigured into an Antwerp moneybags as hard as the precious stones he deals in. I have two mothers. One is Hindele, the beloved storyteller of the *alte heim* and her own mother Bathsheva's castaway. The other is Esther Kreitman, ever Bathsheva's daughter, and as the Yiddish saying has it, *dos epele falt nisht veit foon boimele*—the apple does not fall far from the tree.

Flying bombs, "doodlebugs," strike London. When Hazel tells Lola how these birds without wings stop flying and drop out of the sky to go *boom!* it is time for their evacuation.

On their return I flatter myself that with evergreen memories of my own childhood I am well able to divine Hazel's feelings at the ripe age of three. The conviction has grown on me that, having seen so little of me, she regards me as something of a stranger. One evening, coming home from work, I am met by Lola with dismayed laughter. Hazel went missing for an hour and was found pedaling her red tricycle in busy Finchley Road. What was she doing there? She was on her way to take a bus and ask the conductor to drop her off at Daddy's office. I am enlightened on the depths of my ignorance.

The letter box is a repository for nothing but electricity and phone bills. One day, however, the postman delivers a sealed letter. In it is a call-up paper from the Polish Brigade in Britain, of whose existence I, a Polish citizen, was unaware. I serve Reuters notice of my imminent departure to the wars. The foreign news editor says, "Hold your horses!" He obtains my exemption.

41. END OF THE WAR

The war is at an end. Hitler in his Berlin bunker commits suicide with his mistress Eva Braun. The German Third Reich capitulates unconditionally.

Reuters launches a new enterprise, Atlas Features. Joe Gallagher, who runs it, has read *The House of Napolitano* and *Jewish Short Stories of Today*. He sends me on a trial assignment to Windermere, in the Wordsworth Lake District, to write up the arrival of a group of Yiddish-speaking children from the Theresienstadt concentration camp. They, whose parents "went up the chimney," balk at the sight of the flat-roofed concrete huts in which they are to be quartered, mistaking them for gas chambers and crematoria. I call my piece "Flat Rooftops."

Next I produce a full-length book on the industrial war effort of the Nuffield Organisation. I entitle it *Calling All Arms* and sign it "Ernest Fairfax."

Joe Gallagher engages me as a full-time feature writer and suggests I change my name by deed poll to less of a tongue-twister than Kreitman. Harking back to a reputed ancestor, the Cabalist Yosef Caro, I anglicize him into Carr, change Morris to Maurice, become a naturalized British citizen, and am appointed a roving correspondent based in Paris.

The parting from my mother in London passes off without overmuch pathos. Foyles, the London bookshop and publishing house, has accepted *Deborah*.

42. ANOTHER TRIP TO PARIS

Outfitted in the regulation army uniform of a British postwar correspondent, with the letter *C* on my cap—I'll be mistaken for a colonel—off I go. Lola and Hazel will join me as soon as I have settled into my new duties. Lola will travel light, as I do, with minimal hand luggage. Hazel, who in kindergarten has learned to read, will carry *The Old Nursery Rhymes*, illustrated by Lawson Wood, a big heavy volume. She insists.

For the second time in my sheltered life I step out of the Gare du Nord into Rue La Fayette. Its buildings rise wholly intact, but the once-busy thoroughfare is deserted, ghostly, in the winter twilight.

I take a horse-drawn cab to the Hotel Chatham, close to Place de l'Opéra. There I have a reservation—all its guests are uniformed British—and am ushered into a spacious, well-heated, superbly furnished room with two windows overlooking a quiet street. Attached is a private bathroom. Do I deserve such comfort in what I presume to be a judenrein city? Must I feel guilty at not having also "gone up the chimney"?

After a sound night's sleep and a breakfast of strong black coffee and fresh croissants, I betake myself to the Cafe Thénint on Place de la République. I do not enter. No Yiddish literati. Still upholding an olive sprig of peace high above the rooftops is the bronze dame personifying *liberté*, *égalité*, *fraternité*. For the rest of my stay in Paris, all of twenty years on and off, I shall as far as possible give the Place a wide berth.

I proceed to the Reuters office in the Agence France-Presse building on Rue du Quatre Septembtre overlooking la Bourse, the stock exchange built in the style of a pillared Roman temple. Harold King, the veteran correspondent from Moscow and himself new to Paris, is expecting me. He receives me, a newcomer to journalism, as a colleague on equal terms.

I get down to work and do a piece on the latest fashion of *les Parisiennes*, sporting shoes with high, very high, wooden heels—vertical disavowals of horizontal collaboration. I am commended for my second piece, the report of a visit to an exclusive brothel in town. Its madame takes justifiable pride in her clientele, the high-ranking Allied liberators of the here and now dim City of Light. She bristles somewhat when I enquire about her German clientele during the occupation but is too polite to rebuff a rude young man who should know better.

Harold King takes me to Maxim's for dinner. I have my first-ever taste of lobster—it's *trefa* nonkosher and truly delicious—but I refuse to swallow his account of Stalinist intolerance, totalitarian corruption, foul intrigue, and mass murder in the Communist paradise. I counter with the epic of Stalingrad and incriminate the Western powers, the champions of democracy, who with malice aforethought appeased Hitler, bringing on the most atrocious of all wars.

Harold King shakes his head at me and I do so at him in like despair. Ours is what the French call *un dialogue de sourds*, which later will remind me of the Yiddish tale of two disputants who, to their astonishment, were judged by the rabbi to be each equally and perfectly right.

The day of days dawns. I go to Calais. On the dockside I catch sight of Lola wrapped in a sealskin and Hazel in a bright red coat, *The Old Nursery Rhymes* upheld on both palms, descending the gangway of the ferryboat. I rush to meet them, sprain my ankle, and keep running for hugs and kisses. On their first and my third exit from the Gare du Nord—I hobble—the taxi I ordered is waiting to take us to the Hotel Chatham.

On the morrow I bid them good-bye for a while. From the Gare de l'Est I take the train into Germany to cover the trial of Ilse Koch, the "Bitch of Buchenwald."

My life as an adult has begun.

EPILOGUE, 1991

Much has happened since that summer long ago in a pinewood dacha near Swidow. Most of, but not all of, the Yiddish writers and poets perished in the Holocaust.

The child Yasha died a natural death, of pneumonia, in Warsaw. His father, I. J. Singer, my uncle Shiya, died of a heart attack at an early age in New York. His mother Genya followed. And so did Hindele, my mother, some years later in London.

And now it is my uncle Yitzhak's turn. Of all things it is the remark he made over a rotten egg—"Such, yes, such is life"—in that long-ago summer of 1926 that comes back to me as I stand before a newspaper kiosk in Paris in 1991, staring and being stared at by front-page obituaries in the French morning papers for Isaac Bashevis Singer. The leftist daily *Libération* carries a photograph of him covering two thirds of the front page. The caption in a large red box announces "YIDDISH LOSES SINGER. Isaac Bashevis Singer, the last great writer in the Yiddish language, died Wednesday, aged 87. See page 2." I see page 2 and go on to pages 3, 4, and 5, wholly and reverentially devoted to the Nobel laureate of literature, the Singer who sang the swan song of our *mammaloshn*, the Yiddish mother tongue.

I turn again to the front-page photo, a studio portrait of Bashevis in the pose of a comedian. Against a backdrop of phantoms painted on a screen, he stands holding an umbrella in his outstretched right hand—too far out of line to keep the make-believe rain from his skin-and-bones figure—and wearing sunglasses against the make-believe sunlight. Shabby in an ill-fitting, outsized, expensive suit, with a trilby hat jammed tight on his cranium, he looks tense, though his gaunt face bears a faint smile blending mockery with resignation—the same blend that sets the tone of his masterly novels and short stories.

The paradoxical was the norm for my uncle Yitzhak. He, who always insisted that he did not give two straws for family, adopted the pseudonym *Bashevis* after his mother Bathsheva. Quite exceptional too was the relationship between him and his elder brother Shiya.

But to go back some years. It is 1945. The war is won; among the lost are six million Jewish men, women, and children. I am now working for the Reuters news agency as a roving correspondent in Europe and North Africa and am quartered along with Lola, Hazel, and my mother, who is visiting from London, in the five-star Chatham Hotel near the Place de l'Opera in Paris. One day my uncle Yitzhak arrives for a visit. Climbing the stairs and avoiding the elevator as was his wont, he reaches our landing only to find my mother in hysterics, a malady that has come to afflict her in place of her previous bouts of epilepsy. Ordinarily these fits must simply run their course to the point of exhaustion, but at his command—"Stop upsetting the kinder!"—she recovers her composure.

During this meeting in Paris he gives me some advice as to how to succeed as a writer. It will do me good to find myself a mistress, preferably up on a sixth floor. The exercise of walking upstairs with the blood pulsing more swiftly through my body, and the deceit I shall have to practice on my wife when I go home, will tone me up, keep me out of a rut. Also I should investigate myself to see whether writing comes easiest to me morning or night, lying down, sitting, or standing up.

He has become a vegetarian, partly out of principle but also because he is anxious to not clog himself—the writing machine—with superfluous fats.

"Treat yourself as you would a musical instrument, learn how to play yourself," he says. He is traipsing around with a violin he bought as a gift, but will not deliver for years yet, for his young son living in Israel in a kibbutz.

In December 1967 I have another brief encounter with my uncle at his home in New York. He has aged well, not put on an ounce of flesh. I remember him at age 22 in Swider. He was so thin he seemed unreal. If it had not been for the cold sweat pouring down him he might have been a wraith, he was so remote. His hands were like his voice—terribly soft and fearfully caressing, as if everybody around him were beasts let out of cages and liable to get vicious unless soothed and tamed. Now his red hair is gone from his bulging cranium. My mother used to say that the reason he had that big bulge at the back of his head was that he had a second, double brain. The red has even faded from his eyebrows, and he is no longer bathed in perspiration. He looks more than ever the wraith.

In his soft, deceptively caressing voice, in his fluent English with the broad Warsaw Yiddish accent, he confides to me his current writing technique. Overnight he dreams up in outline what he wants to put down on paper. In the morning, wearing his dressing gown and seated not at his littered desk but on a couch and resting his writing pad on his knees, he goes into a half trance, and the creation flows. He does not mind taking phone calls during these seances. He is able to turn himself on and off at will.

Did my uncle urge me to be a storyteller? Very well; I do now have a story to tell, and here it is. One day, while living in Paris, I am hurrying along the Boulevard de Bonne-Nouvelle, meaning the Boulevard of Good News (this is fact, not fiction), when I suddenly hear the sound of an odd but somehow familiar name, "Jambul"—or do I simply imagine having heard it? I stop short in the busy throng and catch sight of a short, stocky man leaning against a shopwindow, wearing a trilby hat with its brim lowered just enough to leave one eye uncovered. And yes, he is speaking Yiddish to a companion. I go up to the stranger and ask whether he did in fact just say the name "Jambul." His watery eye in its drooping sac looks me over and he nods assent.

Jambul is a place somewhere in Siberia, one of the new towns built by slave labor in Russia's frozen north. My grandparents and my uncle Moshe were deported there from the Galician shtetl that became part of the Russian-occupied zone when Stalin and Hitler partitioned Poland in 1939. At the end of the war my mother received three postcards from her mother in Jambul informing her that Bathsheva and Moshe were there together. To the name of Pinhas Menahem, her husband, my grandmother appended the Hebrew initials denoting "of blessed memory," but where and how he died she did not say. There was never a fourth postcard.

"Were you in Jambul?" I ask the watery-eyed stranger, who again nods in assent. "I have an uncle Moshe Singer who is living there with his mother Bathsheva. Did you happen to meet them?"

"You *had* an uncle Moshe Singer," the stranger half chortles, half snarls. "The *shmoyger* didn't have the gumption to get organized, so he let himself starve and freeze to death. Did his wife hate him! Children? No children. His mother? When I left she was still around, but not for long, I guess."

I do not believe in Satan, but there he stands, incarnate, with only one watery eye showing from the turned-down brim of his trilby hat. I do not believe in predestination, but how else am I to account for these ill tidings recovered that day on the misnamed Boulevard de Bonne-Nouvelle? I walk away, blaming my grandmother Bathsheva for the death of my uncle Moshe, my namesake, and for my own birth.

Uncle Yitzhak, when I tell him of this encounter, listens with bowed head. The muscles of his gaunt face register a tremor. His lips move for words uttered in silence.

* * *

Many years later my uncle Yitzak comes to visit us in Tel Aviv, where we are now living and where we have an apartment on Hayarkon Street overlooking the Mediterranean. He inspects the oil paintings done in two very different styles by Lola and Hazel, lingering over and finally accepting as a gift one of Hazel's canvases depicting a bearded Jew brooding over an empty chessboard. The mood of this visit is a tender one, but the idyll is soon to come to an abrupt, grotesque end.

Some months after this I receive an unexpected phone call. To my surprise Yitzhak is in Tel Aviv again, staying at the Park Hotel, and he wishes me to present myself the following morning at nine o'clock sharp to start work on a joint translation of his newly completed novel. I arrive punctually but have been preceded by Yitzhak's son, Israel Zamir—a reminder that my uncle is also a father.

On my entry Yitzhak motions me to a chair and begins reading aloud from the manuscript resting on his lap. As he reads sentence by sentence, my job is to translate aloud into English without losing the Yiddish flavor. Having no notion of what the next sentence is to be, let alone what story is about to unfold, I begin to flounder, whereupon Bashevis snaps at me, "Simple, simple, keep it simple!"—even as he keeps taking down the sentences I dictate one by one. This goes on for fully two hours, at which point Israel Zamir, cooling his heels and totally ignored all this time, approaches, looms over his seated father, and snarls, "Now I see how you came to write *The Slave*!"

The next day Uncle Yitzhak comes to my apartment unannounced. He sits down at the foot of a couch and, head lowered, hands compressed between his knees, begins brooding. After a longish pause he pronounces judgment: "Your mother was a madwoman." I remind him that my mother was the first of the Singers to take up the pen in Warsaw. But she was, I say, dogged by ill luck, as if truly haunted by the demons she believed in. These so arranged things that at the very moment she was born a black cat threw a litter of kittens at the foot of the bed. Yitzhak agrees.

"God does not bother with the earth we live on; it's just a trivial speck in the universe to him," he says. "He has delegated its management to a petty functionary, an angel with clipped wings, who is a first-class muddlehead and messer. What can you do about it?"

He smiles—a Jewish Mephisto.

He lies on his back staring at the ceiling and throwing off shockers that will get under my skin.

"If a father wants to sleep with his daughter, why shouldn't he? We are all governed by our passions." "Nothing brings two men so much together as sharing the same woman." "If at this very moment Shakespeare, Dickens, and Gogol were playing cards one floor down, I wouldn't bother to drop in. Believe me. Shakespeare would probably turn out to be a drunken sot, Dickens a stuffed shirt, and Gogol a lunatic." "The Jews have a suicidal urge—it runs right through our history."

To this and especially to the statement that my mother was a madwoman, I have a delayed reaction, but a violent one. The following day my uncle is waiting for me outside the Park Hotel where he is being interviewed in Hebrew by a woman journalist, and I walk past him without a greeting. The grimace of pained astonishment distorting his face reminds me of my mother on her deathbed, swinging around aghast to draw her very last breath.

Thinking back on it now, I am a fool for having broken with my uncle Yitzhak. In spite of everything he did dedicate a novel to his sister, though the dedication managed to get her name slightly wrong (Minda Esther instead of Hinde Esther), a misprint he attributed to her *shaidim*—her demons. After all this was over, Yitzhak's wife and ideal life companion Alma, who knew enough to treat him as a storyteller first and last and only incidentally (and discreetly) as a husband, gently remonstrated with me. She wrote a letter explaining that when Yitzhak said wild things he was merely rehearsing possible themes for a story.

The warring personalities inhabiting my uncle Yitzhak's slight frame enriched the compositions, the harmonic flights, of the storyteller Isaac Bashevis Singer. Those literati who foretold, when Yitzhak was still up a tree, that he would "dig into himself" to tap to the full his latent storytelling gifts overlooked the streak of shyness in his makeup that inhibited self-portrayal. More's the pity, for his was a truly fascinating character.

Those literati were wrong as wrong could be in their forecast of an oncoming storm, a cloudburst of Yitzhak's seething resentment against his elder brother Shiya. Yitzhak maintained a compulsive, lifelong posture of worshipfulness toward Shiya, referring to him as "my master" publicly, demonstratively, in and out of season. Here was an enigma, behavior so unlike his customary self or selves—whatever the complexity of his character, submissiveness was no part of it—as to suggest a case of hypnosis. Farfetched? Perhaps, though ultimately Yitzhak did see fit to come out with a confession that not until the lamented death of his elder brother did he he feel altogether free, "free as a bird," to spread his own literary wings.

That Yitzhak Bashevis himself exerted hypnotic powers I can attest, and so surely can many others who found his presence spellbinding. That he himself should have been charmed by Shiya, the melancholy Shiya, and have trod so warily in order never, ever to hurt him, was just one of those anomalies that go to make up the turning, twisted web of life and also the novels and short stories of Isaac Bashevis Singer.

My uncle Yitzhak was not a believer in the betterment of the human species. He voiced his irreproachable philosophy, uttered his ultimate mot juste, over that stinking hard-boiled egg in a sweet-smelling pine-wood forest in Poland: "Such, yes, such is life."

ABOUT THE AUTHOR

Maurice Carr (born 1913 in Antwerp, died 2003 in Paris) was a writer, essayist, translator, journalist, and son of Esther Singer Kreitman and nephew of writers Israel Joshua and Isaac Bashevis Singer. Carr was a Parisian correspondent for the Reuters Agency and editor of *Izrael Magazine*. As a journalist he worked for the BBC, the *Daily Telegraph*, *The Jerusalem Post, Maariv, Haaretz,* and *Commentary Magazine*, among many others. Under the literary pseudonym of Martin Lea, he published the novel *The House of Napolitano*.

whitegoatpress.org